Sarah Blou
mother wl

less than God's best in all areas of her life! This book is full of transparency, vulnerability, and an invitation to come on a journey of fearless parenting. You will be encouraged not only by the words on the page but also by the heart of this book that is found in between the letters. Join her and so many others as you take a journey of learning what it truly means to live out fearless parenting.

—HANNAH OUELLETTE
PASTOR OF THRIVE CHURCH AND FOUNDER OF
FLOURISH WOMEN'S MINISTRY

In the last twenty years the world has changed. With the explosion of technology—computers, phones, etc. plus the erosion of the culture and destruction of the family—it's never been more challenging to raise kids. In her book, *Fearless Parenting*, Sarah Blount deals honestly with the issues of the day and gives positive, practical answers from God's Word to arm you with the tools you need to train kids that are equipped to face the dark world. I believe in Sarah. She is not just giving you theory. I have closely watched her and her husband, busy pastors of a growing church, practice what they are preaching with their three children. I don't endorse this book just because Sarah is my daughter-in-law and I love her. I do so because she is proving that

what she is talking about is working in her own
family. It will work for you too.

—KEN BLOUNT
COAUTHOR OF *DEVIL-PROOF YOUR FAMILY* AND
FOUNDER OF KEN BLOUNT MINISTRIES

Sarah Blount is one of the sweetest ladies you'll
ever meet. But there's so much more to her, and
that's what this book is about. She and her husband, Josh, have learned a few things about parenting that I believe could be revolutionary for
many parents raising kids in today's world. I
wholeheartedly encourage you to dive in and let
God use Sarah's words to encourage and challenge you.

—DELYNN RIZZO, DIRECTOR OF ARC WOMEN

I have known Sarah Blount since she was sixteen years old and have been privileged to have
a ringside seat as God has rewarded her faithfulness by consistently advancing her in the
kingdom of God. Now in her roles of copastor of
New Song Church with her husband, Josh, and
mother of three, I think of Sarah as a rising voice
for her moment in time in the kingdom. She
has keen understanding of this culture and the
challenges and opposition parenting presents
in today's world. I've waited with great antici-
pation for her new book, *Fearless Parenting*.
This is Sarah in her element. She presents practical, life-changing revelations from her dedi-
cated study and love of the Word of God on
this subject. I look forward to the fruit of this

God-breathed project. In my estimation, this is a very timely and important book, a great treasure and must-have for the family.

—TRUDI BLOUNT
COAUTHOR OF *DEVIL-PROOF YOUR FAMILY* AND
COFOUNDER OF KEN BLOUNT MINISTRIES

There are people in life you think you know because they are in your circle of awareness. You see them from afar, view their posts online and watch the greatest hits clips of their life they share. Then there's people in your life that you really know because you've done life with them. You have watched them live out their faith even when it was hard. You saw them get knocked down and not only get back up but do so fighting with their words, attitudes and actions. Revelations 12:11 says "they overcame by the word of their testimony." That is the Sarah that I've known for a long, long time. She is a fierce lover of Jesus that has been modeling Christ follower, spouse and mom to me because of how she lives. This book will sharpen your faith and your desire to be the best parent you can be while doing your most important job: raising children to know, love and serve Jesus with all their heart. I need this book in my life as I navigate parenting my two sons. Sarah, thanks for leading the way, modeling boldness to live out being a fearless parent!

—YANCY
WORSHIP LEADER & SONGWRITER FOR FAMILIES
YANCYMINISTRIES.COM

Raising Godly Kids in
an Ungodly World

FEARLESS PARENTING

All rights reserved

Visit the author's website at sarahblount.com.

Library of Congress Cataloging-in-Publication Data:

An application to register this book for cataloging has been submitted to the Library of Congress.

International Standard Book Number: 978-1-7340760-0-4

Names and identifying details have been changed in some stories to protect the privacy of the individuals referenced.

While the author has made every effort to provide accurate internet addresses at the time of publication, neither the publisher nor the author assumes any responsibility for errors or for changes that occur after publication. Further, the publisher does not have any control over and does not assume any responsibility for author or third-party websites or their content.

Printed in the United States of America

*For Gussy Roo, Peeper Pie, and
Sunny Bunny.*

Being your mom is where it's at.

CONTENTS

FOREWORD

Who will shape your children's future? We live in a society in which multiple sources are promoting their agenda on our kids. At the same time, it can be intimidating to go at parenting alone! But we need not live in fear if we remain vigilant, diligent, and confident.

Sarah Blount's powerful resource, *Fearless Parenting*, addresses these issues with the wisdom of one who was brought up by parents who knew what it meant to raise children according to God's truth. How refreshing to learn from her as she is now passing on that legacy to her own children! As you read, a new level of courage will arise as you discover what it means to raise your children by faith and not by fear. After all, parenting is not a skill we figure out; it is one we must continually hone, as it is the greatest calling on our lives. *Fearless Parenting* will also reveal what it means to partner with the Holy Spirit to train your children to shape culture rather than bow to it.

As first a parent and now a grandparent, I look forward to seeing the fruit these writings will produce in my grandchildren. I invite you to join me and arm yourself with the truth that will take your parenting to another level!

—COLLEEN ROUSE
CO-SENIOR PASTOR, VICTORY WORLD CHURCH

Chapter One

WHY WE CAN'T RETREAT

FOR AS LONG as I can remember, I have loved back-to-school season. I was the kid who, two weeks into summer break, was utterly bored with the *Salute Your Shorts* and *Hey Dude* reruns on Nickelodeon. I was ready to be back in the classroom. I couldn't wait to pick out some new outfits from Mervyn's—some really nice biker shorts trimmed with lace and a matching tunic that would pair well with some fresh, white sneakers from Payless. I can still hear the Payless chime going off over and over again as our big family walked into the store. The most exciting day in August was the one on which I found out who my new teacher would be. And organizing my school supplies was right up there with hearing my favorite song on the radio. Ace of Base, anyone?

I was confident when I grew up and had kids of my own that back-to-school season would be even more exciting, but when the time came to get my five-year-old ready for his first day of kindergarten, excitement was not the emotion I was feeling. Even the giant pencils hanging from the ceiling at Target and tax-free shopping for new shoes, skinny jeans, and mono-grammed backpacks from Pottery Barn Kids could not fill my heart with joy. I was scared. The thought of sending my innocent, pure, Jesus-loving little boy to school—and not just any school but (gulp) public school—made me a wreck.

I grew up in public schools—large public schools with top-ranking sports teams. I was a Tulsa Union Redskin from kindergarten until high school gradua-tion day. I loved it, and I turned out OK, right? So why was the thought of sending my son to public school so hard to wrap my mind around?

Well, let's face it. When you and I were in kin-dergarten, the world was a different place. We had Mervyn's department stores and Toys "R" Us—both now out of business. But that's not all that has changed.

School shootings were unheard of. We had fire drills, and because I grew up in Oklahoma, tornado drills, but we didn't have to practice intruder drills. Our two-week vacation in December was called Christmas break instead of winter break. Because we weren't entirely digitalized yet, we didn't have to deal with cyberbullies. Our teachers simply covered the basics: reading, writing, and arithmetic. There was no need to discuss same-sex marriage, and gender-iden-tity curriculum didn't exist. Our parents didn't have to beg us to play outside; they had to beg us to come inside before dinner got cold.

IT'S A NEW WORLD

The world has changed drastically over the last twenty-five years, and when you're raising kids, you can't help but notice how ungodly the environment is. Kids are killing kids, pornography is a mouse click away, school curriculum is redefining families, children as young as ten years old are taking their own lives, and thirteen-year-old girls are having abortions.

I recently saw a story on NBC about a mom and dad who are raising their three-year-old twins using gender-neutral pronouns such as *they, them,* and *their* to shield them from gender stereotypes. Avoiding the use of gender identification with children is a new parenting trend called "theybies." Parents who follow this trend have decided not to disclose the gender of their children to anyone, including their children. Their hope is that the children can decide for themselves when, if, and how they want to identify as a gender.[1]

My heart breaks when I think about how confused these children will be as they grow up and how far the trend is from the heart of God. I understand parents' not wanting their daughter to feel as if something is wrong with her because she wants to play baseball instead of playing with Barbies, but instead of ignoring the obvious and scientific facts that prove she is a girl, why not teach her that being unique is beautiful? Why not teach her to celebrate how God created her? A three-year-old is barely capable of picking out her pajamas, let alone her gender! At the time of the NBC interview, a Facebook community for parents raising theybies claimed 220 members across the United States.[2]

At least twenty of the fifty United States have had to enact laws about sexting, the practice of sending graphic pictures or video by cell phone, in their legislature.[3] Did you get that? Sexting is so rampant that the government has had to spend taxpayer dollars to write and pass laws to try to prevent it. According to a recent survey, 20 percent of teens have sent or posted nude or semi-nude photos or videos of themselves, and 39 percent have sent sexually suggestive texts, emails, or instant messages. Of the 20 percent who sent or posted nude images of themselves, 15 percent say they did so to someone known only online.[4]

More than 90 percent of young people ages twelve to seventeen use the internet,[5] and 90 percent of eight- to sixteen-year-olds have seen porn.[6] The World Wide Web has arguably become the leading sex educator in our country. Parents used to fear the sex-education class offered by the school system, but nowadays it doesn't seem so bad compared to what they are learning about sexuality from the unrealistic, violent, readily accessible, and dangerously addicting world of pornography.

This is real life, friends. We can't ignore what our children are up against. As difficult as it is not to be shocked by the horrifying statistics I could fill this book with, we shouldn't be. We live in a fallen world that is operating under a curse. What we are seeing is expected. The apostle Paul predicted it in 2 Timothy 3:

You should know this, Timothy, that in the last days there will be very difficult times. For people will love only themselves and their money. They will be boastful and proud, scoffing at God, disobedient to their parents, and ungrateful. They will consider nothing sacred. They will be unloving and unforgiving; they will slander others and have no self-control. They will be cruel and hate what is good. They will betray their friends, be reckless, be puffed up with pride, and love pleasure rather than God. They will act religious, but they will reject the power that could make them godly. Stay away from people like that!

—2 TIMOTHY 3:1–5

Paul pretty much hits the nail on the head, doesn't he? This passage paints an eerily accurate portrait of the days we were chosen to raise children in.

I've heard couples say they don't want to have children because they don't want to raise them in such a broken and confused world. And I have listened to grandparents say they are glad they don't have to raise kids in this day and age. Statements such as these can leave those of us who are on the front lines of parenthood feeling hopeless and fearful. We look around at the selfie-obsessed, sexually confused, entitled, lazy, morally bankrupt, far-from-God culture around us, and because we don't want our children to grow up in it or be affected by it, we retreat in fear. But that's not what God has called us to do.

WE MUST FACE THE DARKNESS HEAD-ON

Since when is it OK for children of God to base their actions on the devastating circumstances that surround us? When did we start believing that the darkness might be able to overcome the light? We must not retreat. We must learn how to tackle issues head-on.

My son, Gus, is right in the middle of his first tackle football season. He has played in some noncompetitive flag football leagues before, but this is our first go-round with shoulder pads, helmets, girdles, and mouth guards. One of the highlights of my summer was seeing him in all his gear. Oh my word. A ten-year-old in shoulder pads—cutest thing ever.

It's been quite a learning experience for him—and me! The first couple of practices, his team worked on activities related to endurance and agility, and he looked like a superstar. But when the time came to practice in full pads, and they brought out the tackling dummies and started hitting, you could tell he was out of his element. All his life he has been told to be careful, slow down, and avoid injury, and suddenly he was being instructed to throw all caution to the wind and run full speed into another human being. He had some major mental blocks. He was getting pancaked by players a lot smaller and weaker than he is. Right before it was time to hit his opponent, he would slow down because he was afraid of getting hurt.

Something finally snapped in him after the first down of his very first game. A freak of an athlete came charging toward Gus, and instead of putting his shoulder down and charging back, he got timid and slowed way down. On impact with the other player, he went flying into the air and came down hard on his behind—thank you, Jesus, that it was not his head!

Gus slowed down and retreated because he didn't want to get hurt, but the slowing down and retreating were the very things that caused him to be injured—and afterward, determined to learn how to tackle. He traded slowing down for full speed! He traded retreating for advancing! He traded fear for confidence, and he's having a really great first season. I see parents retreating in fear all of the time because the world is a scary place, but it's time to stop retreating and start advancing.

As copastor of a growing church plant, I have counseled many mothers who are frazzled, tired, stressed, frustrated, and losing ground. The one thing they all had in common was the fear-based decision they made to homeschool their children. Hear me: I'm all for homeschooling if it's a Spirit-led decision. Some mamas were born to homeschool—they excel at it, and they know how to educate their children while training them to fulfill their God-given purposes. They have the time, energy, and focus to be successful in their endeavors. They feel called and equipped. They are at a place in life where they can devote themselves to being the primary educators of their children. But that was not the case for many of the teary-eyed mothers who sat across from me in coffee shops wondering why they were failing and not enjoying homeschooling.

Wanting desperately to help them, I would ask why they decided to start homeschooling. Ninety-nine percent of the time they would say it was because they were afraid of what their children would be exposed to at school. They didn't want their children to become one of the statistics you read about a few minutes ago. Fear gripped these mothers, and just as Gus retreated from his opponent and ended up getting hurt, they had retreated from the world and ended up hurting themselves, and in some cases, their children. They were getting the wind knocked out of them daily, and their kids were not thriving mentally or spiritually. Some were even rebelling and seeking out ways to do the very things their mothers were trying to protect them from.

Thankfully many of these women were able to trade their fears for faith and start advancing instead of retreating. Some changed their homeschool mind-set and started having more success at home, and some gained the God-confidence needed to send their children to school.

SHELTERING KIDS IS NOT THE ANSWER

I've known parents who refuse to let their teenage children get jobs because they don't want them to be exposed to the "real world." I've known parents who try to keep their children from ever hearing a cuss word. I've known parents who won't let their children watch anything that doesn't involve a singing tomato and a cucumber. I've known parents who think that sheltering their kids from everything is the key to raising great children. But what they fail to grasp is that if their family got stranded on a desert island with no access to secular media, cell phones, friends with bad attitudes, or the internet, sin would still find them. And if their children have not been taught to guard their hearts and to love the Lord with every part of their beings, they are not going to know what to do. And because they will have zero experience in tackling sin, injury will be inevitable.

If our goal as parents is to isolate our children from the darkness that permeates our country, we will fail them. We can't fight off darkness by retreating from it. We fight darkness with light. We need to tackle the darkness head-on and become thoroughly convinced that John 1:5 is true: "The light shines in the darkness, and the darkness can never extinguish it."

Notice the verse doesn't say the darkness will not *try* to overcome the light. We all know from experience that the enemy is persistent and his goal is to snuff out the light of our lives. But God's Word says Satan does not have the wherewithal, the power, or the ability to overcome the light! If we want to fight with light, we need to understand what light is, or better, *who* light is. Light is not some ethereal, Luke-Skywalker-versus-Darth-Vader idea of right over wrong. The light that shines in the darkness, the light that darkness can never extinguish, is a person, and His name is Jesus. He declared this truth along with a promise: "I am the light of the world. Whoever follows me will not walk in darkness, but will have the light of life" (John 8:12, ESV).

LEAD THEM TO THE LIGHT

Instead of asking how we can protect our kids from darkness, we should be asking how we can help them come to love and trust Jesus so they will follow Him all their days. Then they will not walk in darkness. Notice that the verse doesn't say those who are home-schooled will not walk in darkness. Or those who attend Christian school will not walk in darkness. Or those who don't have access to Facebook will not walk in darkness. The verse says whoever follows Jesus will not walk in darkness.

We all know what the culture of the world is like. But what kind of home culture do you have? Are you presenting Jesus to your kids in a way that makes them want to follow Him? Do your kids know Jesus? Not just know *about* Him, but really know *Him*? I have heard my husband say countless times at our church membership class that Jesus does not want to have an *information-ship* with His people. What He desires is a *relationship*.

Jesus didn't die on the cross so we could collect facts about Him or recite historic stories about Him and then someday go spend the rest of eternity getting to know Him better. He gave His life for us so we could know Him right now—like we know our closest friend. Of course we won't even scratch the surface here on earth, but that doesn't mean we should wait until the sweet bye-and-bye to get to know the One who loved us so much He gave His life for us. He wants us to know and recognize His voice,

His character, His presence, His will, His Word, and His plans for our lives.

Paul wrote in Philippians 3:8 that everything else is garbage in comparison with knowing Christ: "Yes, everything else is worthless when compared with the infinite value of knowing Christ Jesus my Lord. For his sake I have discarded everything else, counting it all as garbage, so that I could gain Christ."

Taking your children to church once a week is a great start, but if you think one hour a week is enough for them to get to know Jesus as their closest friend, it's time for a reality check. The more time you spend in someone's presence, the more you get to know them, and the more you get to know them, the more you begin to figure out whether you can trust them.

One of the leaders at our church who oversees our women's small groups is continually studying friendship. She has found that cultivating meaningful friendships is one of the most difficult things for women to do. When women come to her longing for more in-depth relationships, she gives them one tip: consistent, positive interactions. She encourages them to have at least one positive encounter a week with the person they are trying to build a relationship with—whether that involves sending a text asking the person how her week was or taking her out for coffee. She has seen that just one positive interaction a week on a consistent basis will build a friendship that can last a lifetime.

ENCOURAGE MEANINGFUL RELATIONSHIP

If we want our children to have meaningful, in-depth, and lasting relationships with God, we must create consistent, positive interactions between them and God on a daily basis. I'm not talking about simply reading through the classic Bible stories once a year. I'm talking about teaching them to pray and listen for God's voice. I'm talking about worshipping together as a family. I'm talking about breaking down scriptures so they can really grasp them and apply them to wherever they are in life. I'm talking about teaching them how to let God fight their battles. I'm talking about taking the God of the universe and making Him feel like their personal Lord and Savior—because, after all, that's who He is! I'm talking about making this your number one goal in parenting: *Help your children daily experience Jesus and all His goodness so they willingly follow Him instead of walking in darkness.* If you're asking how, I have good news. We'll be talking about what this looks like throughout the book.

I still remember the day we dropped our firstborn off at his big, bad public school. We took obligatory first-day-of-school pictures on the porch. We lived close enough to walk him to school—so we did. We walked him all the way to his classroom. Then we took obligatory pictures with his new teacher. Then we took obligatory pictures of him at his little table. We helped him find his cubby, and then we kissed his baby face goodbye.

What I thought would be a dreadful day full of tears

and hours spent interceding over his soul was actually a joyous day of celebration. What changed? How was the mom who was a wreck just a few weeks before now full of peace and excitement for all that God had in store for her boy?

I met a lady named Jochebed, and I can't wait to introduce you to her in the next chapter. Until then, I've included some questions for you to answer in a small-group setting. You'll find these after every chapter. Get together with some other Christian mamas or couples from your church and dig deeper together. We always grow when we choose to do life with others! So gather your people, and get growing.

QUESTIONS FOR DISCUSSION

1. Do you think the times we are living in right now are more ungodly than they were when you were growing up? In what way or ways?

2. What fears do you have about raising your children in this day and age?

3. Have you ever made fear-based parenting decisions? What were they? How did those decisions affect your children?

4. Do you ever find yourself so consumed with keeping your children from walking in the darkness that you lose sight of the light?

5. If we want our children to have a meaningful and lasting relationship with Jesus, we must create an environment in which consistent, positive interactions are taking place between our children and Jesus. What are some ways you can create that kind of culture in your home?

Prayer for Parents

Lord, I ask You to help me remember what Paul said in Philippians 3:8, that everything else is worthless when compared to the infinite value of knowing Christ. I want to know You better, and I want to help my kids know You better. Give me wisdom and lead me by Your Spirit as I look for ways to create consistent, positive interactions between You and my children. I choose not to retreat. I will advance and be a parent who is taking ground for the kingdom of God. It is my heart's desire to raise children who follow You. Help me not to get caught up in creating perfect scenarios for my children but to focus on stewarding their hearts so that no matter what situations they find themselves in, they will not walk in darkness. I am thoroughly convinced that John 1:5 is true: "The light shines in the darkness, and the darkness can never extinguish it." *In Jesus' name, amen.*

Confession for Children

I follow Jesus, and I will not walk in darkness. Jesus is the Light of the world, and He is the light of my life. The darkness can never put out the light. The most important thing in this life is knowing God. I can know Him as I know my best friend, and that is what my heart desires. I want to know His voice, His character, His presence, His will, His Word, and His plans for my life. I choose to spend time with Jesus daily, because I can't get to know someone if I never spend time with him. I am learning to trust God with everything. I am a child of God, and His Spirit leads me. I follow Jesus, and I will not walk in darkness.

Chapter 2

FAITH OVER FEAR

OR AN EXPECTANT mother, there are few days
more exciting than the day you find out if the
baby you are carrying is a boy or a girl. Whether
you are one of those extremely patient parents who
possesses the ability to wait all the way up until your
delivery day to find out, or if you're like me and want to
know as soon as possible—there's nothing quite like it.

During each of my pregnancies God gave me special insight into the gender of the baby, and of course
He was right every time. But I still counted down the
days to have what He showed me confirmed with
ultrasound technology and a glossy black-and-white
photograph.

Everything always seemed more real after that
moment. Instead of referring to the baby as "baby," we
could begin to call him or her by our chosen name.
The nursery came to life with pretty pastels in shades
of pink or blue. The baby shower plans could com-
mence. I knew exactly what types of clothes I was
looking for when I hit up the sale racks at Baby Gap.

I was expecting all that joy, the happy tears, and a big celebration the day I went to find out if our third child was going to be a boy or a girl, but the morning did not go as expected. We got up early and went to breakfast at McDonald's. The kids played on the big toy as I chugged a cup of orange juice. I wanted to make sure the baby was nice and active for the big twenty-week ultrasound. We made our last predictions and then headed to the doctor's office. Our family of four waited for what felt like hours to head back to the exam room. Everything was behind schedule that morning, which resulted in *Sesame Street* on YouTube and lollipops to keep the kids occupied.

I finally got called back and made myself as comfortable as possible on the exam table. The doctor came in, covered my cantaloupe-shaped tummy with warm ultrasound gel, and began the anatomy scan. My husband had the video camera rolling. We couldn't wait to see the reactions of our three-year-old son and one-year-old daughter. But as the doctor was scanning and telling us about his plans for the holiday weekend, he trailed off. And my husband and I both knew he saw something he didn't want to see. The camera stopped rolling.

Instead of a fun-filled gender reveal, we found out that our baby's heart had stopped beating. I would have to deliver a stillborn child three days later. There were no happy tears, no joy, no celebrating. We were crushed beyond words. The dread of knowing we not only lost a child but also had to gear up for delivering a lifeless baby—how does one wrap his mind around something like that? I imagine Jochebed, the mother of Moses, Aaron, and Miriam (see Numbers 26:59), experienced some of the same emotions during the gender reveal of her third child.

Pharaoh's Plan to Oppress the Israelites

Exodus begins with a death. Joseph, the Bible hero with the coat of many colors who was sold into slavery and ended up becoming the second-most powerful man in Egypt, was gone. God had used the young dreamer to preserve Egypt during a time of famine. Remember Pharaoh's crazy dreams about the fat cows and the skinny cows? Joseph, with his God-given discernment and wisdom, had created a long-term agricultural policy and put some very impressive infrastructure in place that saved an entire nation! Joseph's success in office caused the Israelites to migrate from Canaan and settle in Egypt. But now Joseph and his brothers and their whole generation had passed away. God no longer had one of His own in office; however, His people continued to live in Egypt and grow in numbers. As *The Message* puts it, "The children of Israel kept on reproducing. They were very prolific—a population explosion in their own right—and the land was filled with them" (Exod. 1:6–7).

Joseph was gone, and the pharaoh he worked for was gone too, but the Israelite presence in Egypt was stronger than ever. The new pharaoh was afraid, and the population explosion was causing him to lose sleep. He gathered his people and expressed his concerns: "Look, the people of Israel now outnumber us and are stronger than we are. We must make a plan to keep them from growing even more. If we don't, and if war breaks out, they will join our enemies and fight against us. Then they will escape from the country" (Exod. 1:9–10).

I wonder what Pharaoh's brainstorming session was like. I imagine a room full of fearful leaders throwing out horrible ideas as someone is jotting them all down on a dry-erase board. And finally, after hours of debate and adding to their pros and cons lists, one idea stands out on their dry-erase board and determines their course of action: make the Israelites our slaves.

The first step was to appoint brutal slave drivers over them. The next step was to wear them down with crushing labor such as building cities and storage units. Surely after all this oppression and backbreaking work they would be way too tired to engage in sex. I mean, come on—most married Americans are too tired after a full day at their desk jobs to engage in sex. I'm convinced if someone made Americans slaves in an effort to stop the population from growing, it would work like a charm. But that wasn't the case for the Israelites.

The harder they worked, the more children the Israelites had. There were children everywhere. I'm guessing the Israelite men developed some serious muscles as they lifted heavy stones and worked a sledgehammer all day. The Israelite women couldn't resist. Curls get the girls, right? They were having the most fabulous sex of their lives, and God was blessing them with children.

The Egyptians hated to see that their diabolical plan was not working—it was actually backfiring. So they began to treat the Israelites even worse and made their work harder than ever. But they knew this wasn't a long-term solution. Back to the drawing board and another fearful brainstorming session for Pharaoh and his advisors. Pharaoh knew he had to think bigger. He had to get more creative. He didn't want to annihilate his entire workforce, but he needed to weaken these people. He needed to do something that would stop them from continuing to grow into a race more superior than his own. The idea that the "destroy the Israelites committee" landed on this time? Kill all male Hebrew babies.

Plan A was to order the Hebrew midwives to kill any baby boys born to Hebrew women. But the Hebrew midwives feared God more than they feared Pharaoh, so they did not do what he ordered them to do. Plan B was to put the onus on the entire Egyptian people. Forget the midwives. If we want to see this done, we've got to cut out the middlewoman and do it ourselves. "Then Pharaoh commanded all his people, 'Every son that is born to the Hebrews you shall cast into the Nile, but you shall let every daughter live'" (Exod. 1:22, ESV).

Can you imagine our president ordering us to do something so evil? I don't know anyone who would participate. I think the majority of our country would be trying to get him kicked out of office. But the

Egyptians loathed foreigners. "Hatred of strangers was always a characteristic of the Egyptians."[1] And their hate would drive them to carry out Pharaoh's command. It's estimated that the birth rate among the Hebrews would have been something like eighty thousand babies born every year, or about one hundred males a day.[2] Imagine throwing one hundred baby boys a day into the Nile River! There was no fear of the infant corpses filling the air with an unbearable, putrid odor, because the Nile was swarming with crocodiles that would devour the bodies before decay could set in.

A SPECIAL HEBREW BABY

Joseph was dead. Freedom was dead. Evil was the norm, and sin was fully endorsed by the government. Talk about a horrible time to be raising Hebrew children! Jochebed was right in the thick of it. She was in her third trimester when Pharaoh laid down the law and sentenced all future Hebrew boys to death before they even took their first breath. She was raising her ten-year-old daughter, Miriam, who I'm sure helped look after her little brother, Aaron—at that time probably around three years old.

I can see Miriam waiting on her very pregnant mama and driving her a little crazy by asking several times a day, "How much longer until the baby gets here?" You know how ten-year-old big sisters are: they consider themselves second mothers. I have a brother two years younger than I am. My mom has home videos of me a few days before he was born that show-case me getting his onesies organized and telling my mom how I wanted them folded and stored in his set of drawers. I thought I was his mom until he started school. And then I thought I was his teacher!

I imagine Miriam was the same way. She couldn't wait for her new little sibling to arrive. It would give her something to do. Someone to nurture and care for. Someone to look after. Someone to baby, because Aaron didn't want to be babied anymore; he was growing up. She had always wanted a sister, but now more than ever, she needed the baby to be a girl. Her mom tried to keep her from hearing about Pharaoh's evil plan, but kids talk. So she prayed and prayed for a sister.

Jochebed was right there with her. She tried to think about other things, but every time she felt her baby kick, she found herself wishing, hoping, and praying that she was carrying a girl. There were no black-and-white glossy pictures or ultrasound gels back then. She would have to wait until the delivery for the gender reveal. Usually when a woman is nearing that forty-week mark, she is willing to do almost anything to kick-start labor and get her baby out of her, but Jochebed must have wanted her water never to break. Nevertheless, eventually the time came.

Miriam called the midwife. Jochebed sucked on ice chips. Contractions grew stronger and more frequent. Amram paced the waiting room. Aaron worried about his hurting mama. Jochebed missed the joyful antic-ipation she experienced with her first two deliveries.

The mood was serious. It was time to push, but she didn't want to. She knew the next sentence she heard could be a death sentence. She clenched her teeth, shut her eyes, and gave one final push. The midwife caught her beautiful baby in her arms and with tears in her eyes whispered, "It's a boy."

I imagine those gender-revealing words crushed Jochebed in the same way our unexpected gender reveal moment crushed me. She didn't deliver a still-born baby, but with the new command, her infant boy was as good as dead. No happy tears, no exclamations of joy, no celebrating followed the birth. The thought of her baby boy whom she had been in love with since the moment she found out she was pregnant being drowned and eaten by crocodiles was devastating—how does a mother wrap her mind around something like that?

But wait. That's not how Jochebed's gender-reveal day ended! She opened her tightly shut eyes, took one look at her son, and decided that she would not let Pharaoh write his story. Because "she saw that he was a special baby," she quickly conceived a plan: she "kept him hidden for three months" (Exod. 2:2).

Jochebed saw that her son was special. He was fine, beautiful, fair, goodly, precious, and well-favored.[3] Saying she saw that her baby was special is not saying much at all, if you ask me, because every mother thinks the same thing about their newborn babies. I thought and still do think that my children are fine, healthy, beautiful, and hung the moon. I doubt Moses looked different from any other newborn baby on the outside, but Jochebed could see destiny within him.

She believed that he was born for a reason. God had a purpose for him, and she would do whatever she could to make sure he was able to fulfill that purpose. I believe God had a purpose for every baby born during those days, but blinded by fear, not every parent could see it. Instead of standing up and fighting, they allowed their children's lights to be snuffed out before their time.

JOCHEBED SAVES MOSES

Jochebed whipped out her own dry-erase board and began to think about how she could keep her son alive. She decided the best course of action was to hide him. So she hid him. For three months. For the first few weeks, I'm sure hiding him was relatively easy. Newborns eat and sleep most of the day. With a full tummy, a clean diaper, and a tight swaddle, he probably slept like, well, a baby—maybe in a little cutout in the wall or perhaps a soundproof box that his dad crafted for him.

But after those first few weeks, babies discover how to let you know they are unhappy, and they don't hold back. They cry. Loudly. And they can go from zero to sixty in a very impressive amount of time. One minute they are fine; the next they are screaming because their bottle isn't warming up fast enough. There was no sleep training at Jochebed's house this time around— no option to let the little guy "cry it out." She probably had to be near her son every waking minute, and I'm sure her bond with him grew stronger each passing day. When he turned three months old and starting cooing, blowing bubbles, and pulling back the curtain he was supposed to be hiding under, Jochebed knew she needed a new plan. So "when she could no longer hide him, she got a basket made of papyrus reeds and waterproofed it with tar and pitch. She put the baby in the basket and laid it among the reeds along the bank of the Nile River" (Exod. 2:3).

I know you've undoubtedly heard this story countless times, but I need you to read that again—as if you're reading it for the first time. Go ahead; I'll wait. Don't let your familiarity with this story rob you from seeing what God wants you to see here. This mama got a basket, waterproofed it (without any YouTube DIY tutorials, mind you), placed her three-month-old in the basket, and then placed the basket in the crocodile-infested Nile River.

I literally cannot imagine doing that.

My husband got me a puppy when I was eighteen, and after a weekend spent bonding with the cutest Boston terrier I had ever laid eyes on, Monday came, and I had to put Norah in her crate and leave for work. I cried all the way to the office—over leaving a puppy in a safe crate. A puppy! But a *baby*? In a dangerous, crocodile-infested river? If the crocodiles didn't find him, surely some crazy Egyptian would have no problem tipping the basket over and watching him drown. Jochebed must have been completely terrified, right?

Wrong. So, so wrong. This is the verse that changed it all for me: *"By faith* Moses' parents hid him for three months after he was born, because they saw he was no ordinary child, and they were not afraid of the king's edict" (Heb. 11:23, NIV, emphasis added).

You don't make it into the Hebrews 11 hall of faith with a run-of-the mill kind of faith. You don't get mentioned alongside Noah, Abraham, Sarah, Joseph, Gideon, Samson, David, and Samuel for "sort of" trusting in God. You don't raise a son who gets named in the hall of faith if you don't have great faith yourself. Jochebed possessed a heroic measure of faith. Every decision she made after the birth of her son was a faith-based decision. She hid him in faith. She crafted the basket in faith. She floated him in faith. She chose to ignore Pharaoh's command in faith. She *never* acted out of fear.

Pharaoh, on the other hand, was riddled with fear. All his decisions were fear-based. He was afraid of the Israelites outnumbering the Egyptians. He was afraid they would join forces with his enemies and fight against them. He was afraid of a culture he didn't understand. He was afraid of losing his workforce. And of course, everything he was afraid of came upon him at the hands of the little Hebrew boy whose mama was making faith-based decisions. Her three children led the Israelites out of captivity and the Egyptians to their watery graves.

What a beautiful picture of how faith overcomes fear, every time!

You know the rest of the story. Pharaoh's daughter

found the baby in the basket, and it was love at first sight. Of course Miriam, the miniature mother, was watching over her brother and was right where she needed to be when he was pulled out of the water. She offered to find a Hebrew woman to nurse the baby for the princess, and because Jochebed stepped out in faith, God followed with favor. Jochebed was paid to nurse her own son, and during that time I imagine she talked to him about the God of his forefathers.

We now know that our core belief systems are formed when we are children, possibly during the first six years of our lives.[4] Jochebed would not waste this window. She would take advantage of every opportunity to plant seeds into her son's heart. When he was older and no longer needed to be nursed, Jochebed delivered him to his adoptive mother, the daughter of Pharaoh, who gave him the name "Moses."

Think about how influential Jochebed was in the lives of her three children. She raised one of the greatest leaders the world has ever known in Moses. She raised the very first high priest in Aaron. And she raised the first woman prophet and worship leader in Miriam.

After studying the legacy Jochebed left behind, I decided I was going to be the kind of mother she was. I would be the mom who sees God-given purpose in her children from a young age. I would be the mom who is not afraid of the culture of the world. I would be the mom who does not allow fear to author my children's stories. I would be the mom who takes advantage of every opportunity to instill God's Word in my children. I would be the mom who raises some of the greatest leaders the world has ever seen. I would be the mom whose children light their torches at my flame. I would be the mom who refuses a spirit of fear and opts for a spirit of power, love, and a sound mind instead!

QUESTIONS FOR DISCUSSION

1. Jochebed left a great legacy behind in her three children. What qualities about the life of Jochebed do you admire most?

2. Jochebed knew that God had a special purpose for her son. Do you believe God has a special purpose for your life? Share your purpose with the group.

3. As soon as Jochebed laid eyes on her son, she saw purpose in him. Do you believe God has a purpose for your children's lives? Share anything the Lord has revealed to you about His plans for your children.

4. The favor of God followed Jochebed's decision to step out in faith. Share about a time when the undeniable favor of God followed a faith-based decision you made.

5. Share some belief systems, good or bad, that formed in you during the first five years of your life.

PRAYER FOR PARENTS

Lord, may I be the flame that lights the torches of my children. Help me to leave behind an incredible legacy of leaders. Enable me to think like Jochebed. Help me to make faith-based decisions instead of letting fear author the story for our family. Please show me how to take advantage of every opportunity I have to help my children taste and see that You are good. I pray that every seed I plant in their hearts will produce a harvest. I pray that the time they spend under my roof will help them form the right belief systems. As I step out in faith, I know You will follow with Your favor. I ask You, Lord, to give my children a heart toward the things of God. Help me to see purpose in them and pull greatness out of them. Thank You, Lord, for choosing me to be their parent. In Jesus' name, amen.

CONFESSION FOR CHILDREN

I was born for such a time as this. God has a purpose for my life. I am here for a reason. I will pay close attention to the words of my parents. I will wear them like a crown on my head and rings on my fingers. I believe God chose my parents to be in my life for a reason. I will honor them and come to them when I have questions. My parents can see things in me that I might not be able to see in myself. I light my torch from their flames, and I will make a difference in God's kingdom.

THREE GOD-GIVEN GIFTS FOR PARENTS

I LIKE TO THINK that Jochebed was one of those moms who was blessed with serious chalkboard-lettering skills—which is totally not me, by the way. I have to pay someone on Etsy to create anything handwritten that I want to display. But I'm sure Jochebed was great at calligraphy, and if she were alive today, I bet I know which verse she would have hanging in her family room: "For God has not given us a spirit of fear, but of power and of love and of a sound mind" (2 Tim. 1:7, NKJV).

Such a staple verse in Christian households! I recently surveyed moms on Facebook and asked which scripture they wanted their children to know before they left home, and this verse was by far the most popular answer.

My husband was a pastor's kid, and he jokes about the way he was taught 2 Timothy 1:7. When he was just a little guy, whenever he would wake up scared of the dark or frightened by a bad dream, he would make his way to his parents' room. For some reason, he could never remember which side of the bed his mom slept on, but that was always the side he was hoping to end up on. He knew that if he tapped the covers and his mom rolled over and saw him, he could hop into bed and cuddle with her the rest of the night. But if he tapped the covers and his dad rolled over, he knew he would hear, "Josh, God hasn't given you a spirit of fear. Now go get back in bed."

As I said, 2 Timothy 1:7 is a go-to verse in most Christian households, but something I've seen over and over again is that we focus on just one part of the verse. We focus mostly on what God *hasn't* given us instead of focusing on what He *has* given us.

THE GIFTS WE DON'T OPEN

Imagine it's your child's birthday and you've gone all-out this year. He's entering the double digits, and you're going to make it a birthday he won't soon forget. You have purchased him three incredible gifts that are sure to make all his ten-year-old dreams come true: the latest and greatest video-game system, complete with every age-appropriate game out there; the Bernedoodle puppy he's been asking for since two Christmases ago; and a super-rad four-wheeler. You head into his room and wake him up with breakfast in bed. As he eats his fluffy pancakes, you explain to him that you did not get him a venomous snake for his birthday, but you did get him a video-game system, a Bernedoodle puppy, and a four-wheeler.

You present him with each of his gifts, but he doesn't react the way you are expecting him to. Instead of jumping out of bed and thanking you over and over for the best presents ever, he thanks you only for *not* getting him a venomous snake. He's so distracted by the thing you did *not* give him that he doesn't think to set up his gaming system or pick out a name for his new adorable puppy or strap on his helmet and go for a test drive in his new four-wheeler. He's so hung up on the fact that you did not gift him a snake that he's missing out on the extravagant gifts you *did* give him.

That sounds crazy, but we do the same thing with 2 Timothy 1:7. "God has not given us a spirit of fear." We get stuck on that part. We thank God over and over for not giving us a spirit of fear. But what about what He *has* given us? Are we opening up the gifts of power, love, and a sound mind and plugging them in, creating a space for them, and taking them out for a test drive? Are we so hung up on what He *hasn't* given us that we are missing out on the best part of this verse?

Hear me: The fact that God has not given us a spirit of fear is good news. And you're already way ahead of the curve if you refuse to raise your kids out of a place of fear. The enemy wants to trick you into thinking that being afraid of the world, the American culture, and man is acceptable to God, but it's a trap. First John 4:18 says, "Perfect love casts out fear" (ESV). *All* fear. Perfect love came and made a way for you to be free from all kinds of fear.

Either you believe that or you don't. Either you will keep justifying your fear of the world, or you will realize it is not from God and send it back where it came from. Not having to deal with fear is good news, but here's some even better news: God *has* given you a spirit of power, love, and a sound mind. When you were born again, you received these three amazing gifts. You didn't have to work for them. You didn't have to earn them. You couldn't purchase them. All you have to do is activate them. And if you are going to be like Jochebed, a fearless parent in a scary world, you must understand these three gifts so you'll desire to activate them every day.

Power

Let's unwrap the gift of power and take it for a test drive, shall we? In his commentary Matthew Poole explains what Paul means by the word as used in 2 Timothy 1:7:

> By *power* he [Paul] means Christian courage
> and fortitude, not declining duty because of
> danger threatening us in the performance, but
> enabling us to encounter the greatest dangers
> and difficulties.[1]

Far too many parents are declining their duty to raise kids in the world because of certain dangers that might threaten them in the process. We must go into every day full of courage and fortitude. We must be ready to encounter the greatest dangers and difficulties that come with raising children. We can't dodge this draft. Too much is on the line.

We can't decline invitations to difficult conversations. We can't decline the responsibility we have to train our kids up in the way they should go. We can't decline our God-given duty to raise children who are in this world but not of it. Instead of declining because the pressure is too great, let's be inclined because God's power is greater. May our inclination be boldness, strength, and courage.

Understanding you don't have to parent your children in your own power is a game changer. Trying to do so would be exhausting! It's not you against the world. It's Christ in you against the darkness in the world. And remember, "Greater is He who is in you than he who is in the world" (1 John 4:4, NASB). If you genuinely want to be a fearless parent, that's a promise you must have hidden in your heart.

We can't forget that as we train, sharpen, and eventually release our children into the world, we have all God's power supporting us. I know sometimes the battle between godly kids and our ungodly world feels a lot like the battle between David and Goliath. But remember who came out victorious in that battle? David ran out to meet Goliath in the name and power of the Lord of heaven's armies, and David won! (See 1 Samuel 17:40–51.) Why do we struggle to believe that the same power and the same Lord will join us as we run out to wrestle against the powers and principalities at work in the world? God's power is on your side in the same way it was on David's side.

This gift of power and courage that we've been given is crucial. We can't fulfill our purpose in life without it. We will never reach the people we are supposed to reach if we are afraid of their culture. And our kids will never reach the people they are supposed to reach if they are afraid of their culture. We must stop living afraid and start activating God's power in our lives.

The Bible tells us that after the crucifixion of Jesus, the disciples "were meeting behind locked doors because they were afraid of the Jewish leaders" (John 20:19). They were essentially holed up, isolated, and shaking in their sandals behind those doors! But then Jesus showed up, and things began to change. He ministered peace to them and breathed on them so they received the Holy Spirit. Then right before Jesus ascended to heaven, He told His disciples, "...you will receive power when the Holy Spirit comes upon you. And you will be my witnesses, telling people about me everywhere—in Jerusalem, throughout Judea, in Samaria, and to the ends of the earth" (Acts 1:8).

The Holy Spirit came as promised in Acts 2, and the disciples received power! This was when all heaven broke loose. This was when they came out of hiding for good. They threw away their locks, and instead of shaking in their sandals, they were now boldly standing in front of thousands, proclaiming the gospel, healing the sick, and establishing the church.

That same kind of power is within you right now. *The Holy Spirit wants to empower you with whatever you need to be a great parent today.* No more hiding behind locked doors, wishing things were different. Allow Jesus to breathe on you and fill you with His Spirit. Receive this priceless gift today. Open it up, plug it in, and parent from a place of power.

Love

Even better than a Bernedoodle puppy is the spirit of love that God has given to each of His children. We're familiar with the natural love that exists between most any parent and child, but God is offering us something supernatural here. He has given us the gift to be able to love our children in the same way we love ourselves and to see our children in the same way He sees them. If we want our children to honor us and live long on the earth, then we'll get serious about stirring up the gift of love on a daily basis.

When our children seem to be tuning us out, we can guess why based on Paul's insight: "If I speak in the tongues of men and of angels, but have not love, I am a noisy gong or a clanging cymbal" (1 Cor. 13:1, ESV). Are the conversations you're having with your children laced with a spirit of love? If not, you're going to sound like a clanging cymbal, and anyone in their right mind is going to tune out noise like that. If we want our kids to pay close attention to our words and, as Proverbs 1:8–9 says, wear them like rings on their fingers and crowns on their heads, then we must access the gift of love God has given us.

God allows us to carry His grace and mercy around and dispense it when needed. Our kids are going to mess up, just as we are. The Bible tells us "all have sinned and fall short of the glory of God" (Rom. 3:23, ESV). It has always been that way, and until Jesus returns, that's the way it will always be. But sometimes we forget our kids are human. We forget they were born with a sin nature. We fail to extend grace to them in the very areas in which God has extended grace toward us.

When our kids mess up, are we there to love them through it? I know it can be hard because we have a sin nature too, and our flesh wants to lash out when our children sin—especially when their sin makes us look bad. But we need to love our kids in the same way that we would want someone to love us when we have messed up.

Think about that for a second. When you fall short of the glory of God, how do you want others in your life to respond? I don't know about you, but I feel extremely loved when someone I care about sees me doing something that could hurt me and calls me out on it.

If my husband sees that I'm not disconnecting from work and therefore not resting enough, he will probably say something like, "Babe, I've noticed you're not disconnecting from work. You seem tired and not like yourself. I just wanted to check up on you and make sure you're doing OK and see if there's anything I can do to help." And I will listen (and probably cry) because he's right and I needed that brought to my attention. Then I'll repent and thank God for my 100-emoji husband! That's love.

If he ignored my sinful behavior or made excuses for it, he wouldn't be loving me the way he would want to be loved. If he griped at me or brought it up in front of friends to embarrass me, he wouldn't be loving me the way he would want to be loved. Remember, we are to love our neighbors—and our kids—as we love ourselves.

We all desire to grow, mature, and become more Christlike, and our kids desire the same thing, so the spirit of love has to reign in our households.

One of my favorite phrases to use when we have to discipline our children is a line I borrowed from Moana, the beautiful and courageous Hawaiian leader from the Disney movie of the same name. Moana is on a mission to save her people by restoring the heart of Te Fiti, and the furious lava monster Te Kā is the only thing standing in her way.

At the very end of the film Moana comes face to face with Te Kā, who begins to attack Moana in true lava monster fashion. Moana fights back, but no matter how hard she tries, she is unable to defeat the monster. But then she gets a powerful revelation of Te Kā's true identity. Yes, Te Kā is acting like a monster, but that is not who she is. Te Kā is actually Te Fiti, the beautiful island goddess whose heart had been stolen—the very heart that Moana happened to be holding in her hand, the heart that if restored to Te Fiti would save the island.

Moana calmly begins to walk toward the monster as she sings a song called "Know Who You Are" in which she speaks to Te Kā's actual identity. Her beautiful lyrics assure Te Kā that she not only knows her real name but also that this monsterlike behavior does not define her. Moana restores her heart, and Te Kā transforms back into her true self: Te Fiti, a beautiful, lush, green, and welcoming mountain.

When our kids mess up, or when they are acting like monsters or seem to be pushing us away, we pull them aside and remind them that their mistakes do not define them. They may have acted selfishly, but that is not who they are. They may have been disobedient, but that is not who they are. We remind them that Jesus wants to restore their hearts. We assure them that He knows them by name, and we show them who He says they are in His Word. We remind them of their true identity. Our children respond so much better when the spirit of love is talking to them instead of Mom's and Dad's flesh! As John 6:63 says, "The Spirit is the one who gives life. The flesh doesn't help at all. The words that I have spoken to you are spirit and are life" (CSB).

Don't neglect the spirit of love! Unwrap it over and over again and become a trusted voice in the lives of your children.

Sound mind

If anyone can appreciate the gift of a sound mind, it's a parent. Look at all of the ways the phrase "a sound mind" (2 Tim. 1:7, NKJV) is translated in different English versions of the Bible: self-control (ESV); self-discipline (NIV); sound judgment (CSB); good judgment (GW); soberness of mind (WYC); wise discretion

(Darby); a sensible mind (MSG); a calm, well-balanced mind (AMP).

Yes to all the above, please! I mean, seriously. A sound mind is a remarkable gift many believers have overlooked. What could be more critical as we raise godly kids in an ungodly world than sound judgment, wise discretion, and a sensible mind? Situations will arise that will leave our natural minds stumped, but there is nothing you will ever encounter as a parent that God doesn't know how to handle.

When you are unsure whether your daughter is old enough to date, remember God has given you a sound mind.

When your son brings home a new friend and you wonder about his character, remember God has given you wise discretion.

When you are struggling to find the balance between assuring your kids you love them no matter what their report cards look like and pushing them to give their best effort, remember God has given you a well-balanced mind.

When you find out your son has been looking at pornography, and you want to cry and yell and ground him for life, remember God has given you self-control.

When your sweet ten-year-old has turned into a moody fourteen-year-old and you don't know how to connect, remember God has given you instruction.

When the grind of parenting leaves you feeling reckless, sloppy, mean, slow, tired, and frazzled, remember God has given you soberness of mind.

When you feel as if your child's story isn't adding up, remember God has given you a sensible mind.

When your firstborn gets their driver's license and you're losing sleep, remember God has given you a calm mind.

ABIGAIL: A SOUND MIND AT WORK

We can see the attribute of a sound mind clearly demonstrated by a woman named Abigail who lived during Old Testament times. (See 1 Samuel 25.) The Holy Spirit describes her as "sensible and beautiful"—in that order (v. 3). Yes she was a beauty, but more importantly, she possessed a sensible mind—the same mind God has given you.

Abigail was married to a man named Nabal, who was "crude and mean in all his dealings" (v. 3). David, the anointed king of Israel who had not yet been crowned, sent Abigail's mean and crude husband a message asking him to share provisions with him and his men. It was sheep-shearing season, and David knew Nabal would be rolling in provisions. David's request may seem presumptuous, but David and his men had looked after Nabal's sheep and protected his shepherds, and it was expected that Nabal would return the favor with some food and drink. But Nabal denied David's request, and that did not go over well with David (vv. 4–13).

Word got back to Abigail that David was headed toward her village with four hundred soldiers, swords in hand, ready to kill Nabal and his family and probably anyone else who stood in their way. You don't bring four hundred soldiers along to take out one household! David was so angry that no one could talk him down; no one could get through to him (vv. 13, 21–22).

I love the next part of this story because we get to see Abigail's sensible mind at work. She knew exactly what to do and sprang into action as soon as she heard about the army of outraged young men heading her way. She gathered all kinds of provisions, packed them on a donkey, and secretly headed out to find David. She met him outside town and stopped him in his tracks. He was still fuming and continuing to talk about Nabal's refusal to share with him. Abigail dismounted from her donkey, bowed before David, and began to defuse the situation as she spoke her very calm and sound mind. She apologized—even took the blame—and then talked some sense into David (vv. 18–24).

She told him, "When the Lord has done all he promised and has made you leader of Israel, don't let this be a blemish on your record. Then your conscience won't have to bear the staggering burden of needless bloodshed and vengeance. And when the Lord has done these great things for you, please remember me, your servant!" (vv. 30–31).

David received every word and then thanked her for her good sense:

> Praise the Lord, the God of Israel, who has sent you to meet me today! Thank God for your good sense! Bless you for keeping me from murder

and from carrying out vengeance with my own
hands. For I swear by the Lord, the God of
Israel, who has kept me from hurting you, that
if you had not hurried out to meet me, not one
of Nabal's men would still be alive tomorrow
morning.

—1 SAMUEL 25:32–34

Abigail saved not only countless lives with her sensible mind but also God's purposes and plans for
David. Highlight this truth: *a sound mind can save
my children's lives and preserve the purposes and
plans God has for them.*

Great news, parents! God has not given you a spirit
of fear; He has given you a spirit of power, love, and a
sound mind.

QUESTIONS FOR DISCUSSION

1. Have you been focused more on what God has *not* given you (the spirit of fear) than on what He *has* given you (a spirit of power, love, and a sound mind)? If so, why?

2. Share some of the ways you think having the spirit of power would help you as you raise your children.

3. Did your parents raise you in a home in which the spirit of love was in operation? Consider sharing how the spirit of love or the lack thereof in your childhood home has influenced the way you are raising your children.

4. Sarah explained that we need to love our children the way we love ourselves. In which areas of parenting are you excelling at loving your children as you love yourself? Which areas do you feel need improvement when it comes to loving your children as you love yourself?

5. Share how possessing a sound mind has helped you in your parenting journey. What current situation has your natural mind stumped or perhaps reeling? How can you tap into the sound mind you've been given to successfully work though that situation?

Prayer for Parents

Lord, I thank You that You have given me not a spirit of fear but a spirit of power, love, and a sound mind. Help my spirit to be aware of these amazing gifts so I can tap into them every day. When I feel weak and weary in well doing, I will call upon Your power. I remember that the Greater One lives in both me and my kids. I am full of courage and fortitude. I will not back down when the pressure of raising kids seems overwhelming. Oh, Lord of heaven's armies, I am inclined to boldly stand my ground and fight for my kids in Your name. I will love my children as I love myself.

Help me to be like You, Jesus. Help the words I speak to be full of spirit and life. Help me to remember that my flesh accomplishes nothing. I will be a parent who is led by the Holy Spirit and who reminds my children of who they are in Christ. I will not avoid discipline, because I know that isn't love, but I will discipline as You discipline me. I am in possession of a well-balanced, calm, sensible, sound, and sober mind. I will be like Abigail— I will know how to respond in high-pressure situations. I will have the right words to say. I will be a vessel that helps my children stay on the path You have for them. I have good judgement, and my children will thank me for preserving the purposes and plans God has for them. In Jesus' name, amen.

CONFESSION FOR CHILDREN

God has not given me a spirit of fear. I don't have to be afraid of anything! But He has given me three amazing gifts. I have been given a spirit of power. I am bold and courageous, and I will stand my ground. I do not give in to temptation, because the Greater One lives in me. I have been given a spirit of love. I love others as I love myself. I am quick to extend mercy and grace to others in the same way Jesus is quick to extend mercy and grace to me. I have been given a sound mind. I make good decisions. I know how to respond in times of pressure. I have self-control. My mind is calm and balanced. I have not been given the spirit of fear; I have been given a spirit of power, love, and a sound mind.

Chapter 4

TRAINING UP "LEAN(ING)" MACHINES

I AM THE MOM who cries when her babies receive shots at the doctor's office. Contrary as it may seem, I'm also the mom who gets her kids vaccinated! (Insert shocked emoji face here.) I hope we can still be friends.

When my son, Gus, was three, I took him to the dentist for a checkup and found out he had eight cavities. Yep, you read that right—*eight*. I promise I take good care of my children; I just had no idea that a preschooler was not ready to wield a toothbrush on his own or that the folks who make the bunny-shaped, gummy fruit snacks were in cahoots with the people who make the budget-crushing, cavity-filler material. Those fruit snacks were his jam, but when I received the bill for the eight fillings, they were banned permanently from the Blount family pantry.

I wasn't at the dentist's office when Gus got all those cavities filled. I asked my husband to take off work for the appointment so I didn't have to see my little buddy all gassed up or in pain. I would have been a blubbering mess. Shots, root canals, scraped knees, or hurt feelings—mothers do not like to see their children in pain, physically or emotionally. It's part of our genetic makeup!

If you have a child under the age of ten, chances are you've seen the movie *Storks* close to a hundred times. One of my favorite scenes in the film is a sequence of caring mamas throughout history defending their babies all while REO Speedwagon's "Keep On Loving You" plays in the background. A club-toting mother from the Stone Age protects her baby from a saber-toothed tiger. A toga-wearing mama from the Roman era shields her baby from swords and a spiked ball and chains. A bonnet-clad mother keeps her baby safe from flaming arrows during the pioneer days. Who can relate?

THE INSTINCT TO PROTECT

Our instincts to protect and shield are very real. I remember the day after my firstborn took his first breath. I would doze off in my hospital bed and then wake up a little while later feeling panicked and needing to set eyes on my new little bundle of joy. After I could see that he was alive and well, I would doze off again, only to repeat the panicked wake-up routine a few minutes later. I asked my nurse what was wrong with me, and she explained that my motherly instincts had been activated and were working overtime.

The drive to protect our children is not limited to women. My husband, Josh, didn't sleep a wink the first forty-eight hours after Gus was born. And it had nothing to do with the insanely uncomfortable pull-out bed offered to him. Even when Gus was swaddled, freshly changed, nice and full, and sleeping soundly, Josh couldn't relax. He had to know his new little boy was being looked after, no matter the cost.

Like the women in the *Storks* sequence who were shielding their babies, we do our best to shield our kids from anything that might cause their hearts to ache. I believe this is normal. I believe our instincts to shield and protect our children were passed down from our heavenly Father. After all, Genesis 1:27 says we were created in God's image, and God protects what is precious to Him.

Psalm 28:7 tells us, "The Lord is my strength and my [impenetrable] shield; my heart trusts [with unwavering confidence] in Him, and I am helped; therefore my heart greatly rejoices, and with my song I shall thank Him *and* praise Him" (AMP). This verse and many others tell us that God protects His children by *being* their shield—and not just any shield but an impenetrable one. Yes and amen to that!

WE HURT WHEN THEY HURT

The pain we feel when our kids hurt was also inherited from our heavenly Father. A beautiful lyric in Stuart Townend's song "How Deep the Father's Love for Us" always reminds me of God's caring nature. It refers to the moment when Jesus was dying on the cross and the Father had to turn His face away from His Son's suffering. Jesus must have sensed the loss of His Father's gaze, because He cried out from the cross, "My God, My God, why have You forsaken Me?" (Matt. 27:46, NKJV).

I envision God's looking down upon His one and only Son, who has been beaten beyond recognition and is slowly being crushed by the weight of every evil. The Father's heart is breaking into a million pieces, and unable to see His Son hurt like that, He has to turn his face away.

The night we checked into the hospital to deliver our second son, Felix, stillborn, my doctor explained to us before I was induced that because of the cystic tumor, or hygroma, on his neck—which was what had caused his death in the womb—he would not be pretty to look at. But he said if I wanted, I could hold him, and they would take newborn pictures of him for me.

The night before the delivery, God gave me a dream. I saw a perfect, little, brown-haired, brown-eyed boy in heaven—I knew it was Felix, and that was the image of him I wanted to remember. When it was time to push, I turned my face away and closed my eyes as tightly as I could. I didn't want to see what had hurt him and caused his life to be cut short. I tried to avoid it at all costs.

Just like our Father, we hurt when our kids hurt, and we desire to shield and protect them at all costs. But what happens when we can't? What do we do when our shield isn't quite big enough? How do we

53

deal with situations that cause our kids to experience the guaranteed heart-ache that comes with living in an ungodly world?

WHEN HEARTACHE HITS

In October 2016 I got a fun little surprise in the form of two pink lines. I was pregnant! We had just packed away the crib and decided to wait another three or four years for the final installment of Blount children, so I was shocked but thrilled at the same time. I love being pregnant. I'm really good at being pregnant. If I had a superpower, it would be carrying and birthing ridiculously cute babies. I've been pregnant 140 weeks of my life, and I enjoyed every moment during those 140 weeks. I was ready to add forty more to that number and was immediately starry-eyed thinking about the new Blount baby I would get to meet the following summer.

I knew our kids' excitement would be through the roof when we shared our news with them. I took two blood tests to confirm, and the doctor said my levels looked great and that he would see me in nine weeks. I was already showing. Baby number five don't play; I popped out and popped out fast! I knew I couldn't wait nine more weeks to tell our friends and family, so about two weeks after we found out, I planned a big scavenger hunt that ended with a little video in which we revealed that a new baby would be joining our family in June.

When the video ended and the kids realized what

was going on, pure joy filled our kitchen. I have never seen happiness hit my kids like that before, and you should know they are very happy kids who have had a very happy, Disneyland-filled life. But this baby was something they had been asking for and praying for and thinking about for a while. Our oldest child cried genuine tears of joy. Our middle child jumped up and down and squealed for a good five minutes straight. And our youngest just kept hugging everyone. She didn't know why we were celebrating, but she wanted to celebrate with us. It's a moment I'll never forget even though I blew it and did not hit the record button on my phone to capture it all on video.

The new baby was all my kids could talk about. The papers they brought home from school had drawings and notes on the back of them about their new brother because they had already decided it was going to be a boy. They had to say good morning and good night to my puffy tummy. And they prayed sincere prayers, asking God to help the baby grow big and strong and healthy.

Three days of celebrating came to an abrupt halt after I miscarried. As shocked as I was to find out I was pregnant, I was even more shocked to miscarry. As you know, my third pregnancy ended when I had to deliver our son Felix stillborn. After that, I prayed and believed and trusted God that I would never lose another baby again. And I was convinced I wouldn't. But I did.

Of course, I was heartbroken over the loss of life, but the thing that hurt the most was knowing that I was going to have to tell my kids. There was no way around this: *I would have to watch their hearts break.* I was so angry with myself! Why? Why didn't I follow the pregnancy announcement protocol? Why didn't I wait longer to tell the kids? I could have saved them. I could have shielded them. I could have kept them in their bubble.

Show Them How to Overcome

I'll never forget sitting in my kitchen the afternoon of the miscarriage, sorting out bingo cards for a party at my kids' school that I was in charge of hosting later that day, my eyes blurry from all the tears. I knew that in just a few short hours, after school was over, we were going to have to sit the kids down and let them know that life isn't perfect. As I punched out Charlie Brown bingo markers and beat myself up for seemingly jumping the gun with the pregnancy announcement, the Holy Spirit came and did what the Holy Spirit was sent to do. He comforted me with these words: "You can't always shield your kids from heartache, but you can show them how to overcome." In other words, what's done is done. You can't protect them from this one, but you can use this situation to help them see that the Greater One lives in them, and because of that, they can find victory in the midst of a terrible loss.

After I painfully smiled my way through the class party and got the kids home from school, we sat them down in the living room and broke the news. They wept and moaned and cried for what seemed like an eternity. Josh and I cried with them and held them and let them cry until they were ready to talk. They were so confused. How could this happen? Why did this happen?

I didn't feel equipped to answer those questions because honestly I didn't know how and why it happened, and I still don't. It still doesn't make sense. But at that moment we told them what we *did* know: God is faithful, no matter what. God never leaves us or forsakes us. God will heal our broken hearts. God will turn this sad story into a happy one.

We stayed in our living room for hours that night and talked about heaven and the hope we have in Jesus. What I thought would be one of the worst nights of my life ended up being one of the best because that night I got to see that my two older children's faith in God was immovable, even in the midst of a storm. Their five- and eight-year-old hearts held tightly to the promises of God. The Jesus they had always sung about and read about and talked about became even more real to them that October night.

When Jesus was on earth, He warned, "Here on earth you [that includes me, you, my kids, your kids] will have many trials and sorrows"—but then assured us, "take heart, because I have overcome the world" (John 16:33).

When our kids face real-life challenges, we often try to shield them from as much pain as possible. We don't want them to have to experience hurt feelings, rejection, not making a sports team, the death of someone they love, disappointment, or anything else that would cause their little hearts to hurt, but sometimes we shield them from too much, and they grow up never getting a chance to lean on God entirely.

TEACH THEM TO LEAN ON JESUS

Proverbs 3:5 instructs us to "trust in the Lord with all [our] heart and lean not on [our] own understanding" (NIV). We can't expect to stop leaning on our own understanding if we live in a world where everything makes sense, and I'm concerned that's the kind of world we try to create for our children.

We must come to terms with the fact that trying to make this crazy, mixed-up world we live in make sense is futile. Our children need to know we live in a fallen world and that the trials and sorrows they face won't always make sense to their natural minds. Not understanding is absolutely OK—as long as they lean on Jesus and allow Him to minister to their hearts the incredible peace that goes beyond our understanding.

Leaning is a crucial posture for living the glory-to-glory life that the apostle Paul talks about in 2 Corinthians 3:18 (NKJV)—so crucial that he commended the church in Colossae for having it. Please read what he has to say in the following verse slowly and intentionally. (No skimming!) Pay attention to every word and then reread it. Ask yourself whether it describes the way you lean.

> For we have heard of your faith in Christ Jesus
> [the leaning of your entire human personality

on Him in absolute trust and confidence in His
power, wisdom, and goodness] and of the love
which you [have and show] for all the saints
(God's consecrated ones).
—Colossians 1:4, ampc

That is how I want to lean! With my entire human
personality. With every fiber of my being. With the
full weight of my mind, emotions, body, and spirit
leaning on Jesus in absolute trust and confidence.
Notice that the people Paul was commending were
leaning in absolute trust and confidence not on their
own power, wisdom, and goodness but on the power,
wisdom, and goodness of Jesus!

When we put our trust and confidence in our own
might, understanding, and good deeds, we will fall
flat on our faces. We were not designed to support
the weight of the world in our own strength. "You
are enough" is a lie many well-meaning ministers
are feeding people today, but the actual truth is you
are *not* enough. It is vital that we realize this truth
because the moment we come to terms with the fact
that we are not strong enough, intelligent enough, or
good enough, we'll begin to lean entirely on the One
who actually *is* enough!

It's in Christ that we live and move and have our
being because Christ *is* enough! Don't get me wrong,
you're great, but it's only because the Greater One
lives in you.

I've made the mistake of putting my trust and confidence in something that wasn't designed to support

the weight of my entire being before—it wasn't fun. I was checking kids into a classroom at church, leaning with my full weight against a dinky white baby gate that was "secured" in the door frame. It couldn't handle my 5'4" 105-pound self leaning against it. The gate gave out, and I ended up sprawled out in the hallway with carpet-burned knees and a severely bruised ego. Our power, wisdom, and goodness in comparison to God's are like that dinky, white gate. We've got to stop leaning on our own understanding and start leaning on the immovable Rock of Ages!

When our kids see us leaning on Christ as the church of Colossae did, they will follow suit—*if* we give them a chance to. If you want to raise God-dependent leaning machines, you've got to present them with opportunities in which you don't provide all the answers—you don't try to make everything make sense. You don't come to their rescue and make it all better. You're going to have to let them face some challenges—a difficult thing for parents to do. Remember those God-given instincts to protect and shield? But if we want our children to know what it means to trust God from an early age, we have to let them exercise that trust.

Look to Jesus and the Holy Spirit

Jesus was great at giving His disciples opportunities to exercise their faith. He let them face some storms. He made Peter step out on the water when He could just as easily have met him on the boat. (See Matthew

14:28–29.) He didn't allow them to sit back and watch as He fed the five thousand; He made them participate. (See Matthew 14:13–21.) Jesus wasn't in the business of bailing people out or preventing them from ever facing difficulty; He was in the business of teaching people to lean on Him in every situation. He wanted to mature the faith of His disciples, so He made sure they had plenty of chances to use it. What a great model for parents!

Romans 8:14 tells us that "all who are led by the Spirit of God are children of God." Are you a child of God? Then you can be led by His Spirit! Ask the Holy Spirit to help you be alert to opportunities to encourage your child to lean on God. Be sensitive to His leading and steward well every opportunity that presents itself. Work may be pressing. Your cell phone may be chiming. Dinner may be burning. Ignore it all if you see an opening to partner with the Holy Spirit and position your child to lean wholly on God.

You also need to have routinely scheduled time with your children—so routine that your kids know when to expect it. Our two oldest kids start school one hour later every Wednesday, so my husband and I alternate taking one of them out to breakfast on Wednesdays. They know they get one breakfast date with mom a month and one date with dad a month—one-on-one time during which they can talk to us about anything and we'll listen and allow the Holy Spirit to lead us.

If they bring up some frustration with a friend, we don't call the friend's parents and try to fix everything for them. We direct them to God's Word and connect them to His voice. We aren't looking to bail them out or solve all their problems. Our goal is to get them to lean on God and allow Him to direct their paths.

There is an entire generation of parents out there today who don't know Jesus as their personal Lord and Savior because their moms and dads acted as middlemen between them and God. They never had a true, intimate connection with the Trinity. What if we cut out the middlemen and start allowing our children to take ownership of their relationship with God? What if we let them face some challenges? What if we stop trying to shield them from every single thing and start giving them opportunities to put their trust in the Lord? We would raise the fiercest generation of sons and daughters the world has ever seen! A generation who knows how to get back up when they get knocked down. A generation whose faith in God is real, tested, and unshakable. A generation who knows where to turn when the wind and waves come. A generation full of sure-footed, steady-handed, battle-worthy conquerors.

The last thing my eight-year-old said to me the night we told him about the miscarriage was, "Mom, this has been the saddest day of my life...but I will never stop trusting God."

If there are no rough roads to walk, no mountains to climb, and no battles to fight, our children miss out on the God of John 16:33, the God who has overcome the world. Love, protect, and defend your children, but more importantly, teach them to lean on God so that He can display His glory in their lives now and forever.

QUESTIONS FOR DISCUSSION

1. "You can't always shield your kids from heartache, but you can show them how to overcome." What do those words that the Holy Spirit used to comfort Sarah mean to you?

2. Would you say that the verse in Colossians 1:4 about leaning with your entire personality on God describes you? Would your kids describe you as someone who leans not on his own understanding but trusts in God? Why do you think it's important for our children to witness our leaning and depending on God?

3. What does your routinely scheduled time with your children look like? Share what works for your family and how you might improve on it.

4. Did you experience a middleman relationship with God when you were growing up, or did your parents work to connect you personally with God the Father, Jesus, and the Holy Spirit? How can you ensure that you are raising children who are not just riding on the coattails of mom and dad's walk with God but who take ownership of their personal walk with God from a young age?

5. Do you tend to bail your children out or try to fix their problems for them? How has this hindered them? What action steps will you take to present your children with opportunities to grow their faith?

PRAYER FOR PARENTS

Father, thank You for showing me how to lean. May the words Paul used to describe the church of Colossae be words that my family and friends use to describe me. Help me to lean not on my own power, wisdom, and goodness but to confidently lean on Your power, wisdom, and goodness. You are enough. You are an immovable rock, and when things don't make sense, I choose to lean on You. Help me to be a Spirit-led parent. I ask You, Holy Spirit, to help me see opportunities to connect my children to Your Word and Your voice. Help me to steward well every opportunity You place in front of me. Lord, I commit to raise children whose faith in You is real, tested, and unshakable. In Jesus' name, amen.

CONFESSION FOR CHILDREN

I am a leaning machine. I don't lean on my own understanding, but I lean on God. It's OK when things don't make sense, because Jesus gives me a peace that goes beyond my understanding. My God is full of power, full of wisdom, and full of goodness. He's a rock that can't be moved. I am a leaning machine. I know how to get back up when I get knocked down. My faith in God is real, tested, and unshakable. I know where to turn when the wind and waves come. I am a leaning machine.

Chapter 5

HOW WE ARE TO VIEW OUR CHILDREN

I AM A CHURCH kid through and through. My parents had me at church when I was just six days old, and I can count on one hand the number of times we missed a service. We were there every Sunday morning, every Sunday night, and every Wednesday night. I am forever grateful for my mom and dad's love for the local church.

I received a strong foundation in God's Word in children's church and through programs such as the Missionettes. By the time I finished elementary school I knew every Bible story that was memorable enough to have a coloring page to go with it—including the one about God's appearing to King Solomon and saying to him, "'Ask for whatever you want me to give you'" (1 Kings 3:5, NIV). I was always disappointed with Solomon's answer: "a discerning heart" (v. 9, NIV)— essentially, wisdom.

Wisdom? If the God of the universe had showed up in my youth and told me to ask Him for whatever I wanted, wisdom wouldn't have even cracked my top-ten list. It would have been more like a date with Jonathan Taylor Thomas, a massive mansion for my family, all the rare Ty® beanie babies, a huge vault overflowing with gold coins that I could jump into—like on *DuckTales*—and world peace. But now that I'm not a fifth grader, I see that wisdom was an excellent choice.

God thought so too. He gifted Solomon with wisdom and also threw in wealth, possessions, and honor. Solomon was considered to be the wisest man who ever lived. He possessed unique insight that no one else had, and Solomon is the man the Holy Spirit chose to write the verses that we are going to be digging into in this chapter.

CHILDREN ARE A GIFT FROM GOD

In Psalm 127:3 Solomon wrote, "Children are a gift from the Lord; they are a reward from him." He offers us a godly perspective of our children: they are a *gift*. Jochebed knew that full well. When she laid eyes on Moses, she knew he was not a burden or a mistake but a precious gift from God full of unlimited potential. How do you view your children? Maybe you're in a season in which you need to be reminded that your son or daughter is just as much a gift from the Lord as Moses was to Jochebed.

I know children don't always feel like a gift. Let's be honest: a lot of times they feel like a burden. We have to get up early and take them to school. We have to stay up late packing their lunches and making sure they did all their homework correctly. We have to take them to the restroom right when our food comes out at the restaurant. We have to clean up the hallway when the tummy bug hits and they don't quite make it to the barf bucket. We have to change their diapers for two, sometimes three years. We have to make them dinner and then beg them to eat it. We have to pay a babysitter when we want to go somewhere without them. We have to chauffeur them to after-school practices. We have to make sure they brush their teeth and buckle their seat belts. We have to basically help them survive every single day. Parenting is a twenty-four-hour-a-day job with no vacations, no overtime, and no pay.

With so many tasks both physical and mental related to parenting, it's very easy to begin to view our children as grievances instead of gifts. And though raising children can be difficult, stressful, and very inconvenient, the fact remains that children are a gift from God.

Every parent has his or her convictions when it comes to birthday party etiquette. But if my kids are having a party and guests have gone out of their way to bring presents, you better believe my kids will be opening those gifts in front of everyone at the party. And upon opening each gift, they will be making eye contact with whoever brought the gift and sincerely thanking them; or better yet, they will leave the present-opening station to give the person who brought the gift they just opened a giant thank-you hug. Yes, it takes forever to open gifts this way, but I want my kids to be thankful, and I know we won't get around to sending thank-you cards after the party is over.

I have a feeling God is waiting on several thank-you hugs from parents who have forgotten that every day with their children is a gift from Him. If we are viewing our children as annoyances or burdens, chances are we aren't thanking God for them. When was the last time you thanked God for an annoying fly that was too quick for your flyswatter? Never, I'll bet. We don't thank God for things that inconvenience us!

When you see your children as burdens, they will believe they are burdens; and if they believe they are burdens, they will act like burdens. It's a vicious, ugly, unhealthy cycle. But if you see your children as gifts, they will believe they are gifts; and if they believe they are gifts, they will act like gifts. It's a sweet, beautiful, life-giving cycle. Which cycle are you in?

Seeing our children for the gifts they are also connects us with the Gift-Giver. Every time I'm reminded that God picked me to be the mom of Gus, Beau, and Sunny Blount, the thought of that privilege makes me love Him even more. And the way we were designed to express our love to God is through thanksgiving and praise.

Now, think about this: According to Psalm 100:4, it is with thanksgiving and praise that we are to enter into God's throne room—and it is there in His presence, Psalm 16:11 assures us, where we find fullness of joy. No matter how trying a day you may have had with your children, before you fall asleep, remind yourself they are a gift and begin to worship God for them.

Before you know it, you'll be in His presence, at His feet, exchanging your frustration for His joy. And His joy will provide you with the strength you need to start over tomorrow morning.

CHILDREN ARE ARROWS IN OUR HANDS

Besides declaring that children are a gift, Solomon goes on to say in Psalm 127 that children are like arrows. "Children born to a young man are like arrows in a warrior's hands. How joyful is the man whose quiver is full of them! He will not be put to shame when he confronts his accusers at the city gates" (vv. 4–5).

There is so much depth in this analogy about children and arrows. It's only a few sentences, but those sentences are full of God-given wisdom intended to instruct parents on how to view their children and what to do with them during the eighteen or so years they are living under their roofs.

I'll be honest. Before studying this verse, I knew nothing about arrows, except what I learned from watching the Disney movie *Robin Hood*. I've never shot a real arrow. I've never even held a real arrow. These days they aren't ordinary, everyday objects—I mean, sure, arrows have been trending on Etsy for the last three years, but this verse isn't talking about décor; it's talking about weapons.

When Solomon wrote Psalm 127, arrows were common in civil and military life. Arrows in the hand of a skilled warrior were not just any weapons but the weapon of choice. The bow and arrow outperformed the javelin, the spear, the ax, and every other weapon available in biblical times—and looked exquisite doing so.[1] The type of bow and arrow warriors used required first-rate craftsmanship and could not be produced in mass quantities. This should clue us in to an important truth: Effective parenting—the kind of parenting that can outclass any weapon formed against our children—can't be mass produced on an assembly line. We can't afford to simply go through the motions; great parenting requires first-rate craftsmanship.

First-rate craftsmanship used to be a way of life; now it's a lost art. At the beginning of the twentieth century admiration of stunning craftsmanship began to shift. Quality was no longer king. Now, it was all about efficiency. Enter assembly lines. Sure, the lone crafter created longer-lasting and more beautiful pieces than anything coming off the factory line. But the factory line resulted in cheaper labor and faster production, and that was a trade-off our country was willing to make. We are inherently impatient people.[2]

It seems many parents today are sacrificing quality for efficiency when it comes to raising their children. Instead of purposing to keep in step with the Spirit as they nurture the gifts God has given their children, they resort to assembly-line parenting.

Assembly line parenting asks, How quickly and cost-effectively can I turn this child into a successful adult? These parents think if they start at the beginning of the line and continue to push their children from one workstation to the next, then in about eighteen years a fully assembled adult will be produced. Hopefully their kids won't bother them too much along the way, but if they do, they can always put a smart device in their little hands to keep them occupied.

Parenting is not a turnkey operation. We often think if we can enroll our kids in a great school, give them ample opportunity, attend church regularly, and have dinner as a family three times a week that we are guaranteed to produce quality adults, but that's not how it works. If you want a quality child who grows into a quality adult, you're going to have to commit to reclaiming the lost art of craftsmanship.

Jiro Ono, chef at what is considered the best sushi restaurant in the world and the first establishment of its kind to be awarded the coveted three-star Michelin rating, offers insight into how masters of their crafts think. "Once you decide on an occupation, you must immerse yourself in your work," he said. "You have to fall in love with your work. Never complain about your job. You must dedicate your life to mastering your skill. That is the secret to success...and the key to being regarded honorably."[3]

Parents, I pray you fall in love with your work—not your day job but the work of raising your children. I pray that instead of complaining about the long hours, you would see the importance of investing your time and energy. I pray that you dedicate your life to mastering parenting skills—read books on parenting, attend parenting seminars, study what the Scriptures say about it, and ask the Holy Spirit to help you be the best parent you can be for each of your children.

I was struck by the fact that Chef Ono said immersion,

passion, and dedication are the keys to being regarded honorably, because the only command given to our children in Scripture is that they would honor their parents. When we choose craftsmanship parenting over assembly line parenting, honor will more naturally flow from our quality arrows!

I find it interesting that arrows are made up of three main parts, just as our children are. An arrow consists of an arrowhead, a body, and a tail; a child, like all other humans, is made up of a mind, a body, and a spirit. We can learn a great deal about raising our children by comparing the three parts that make up an arrow to the three parts that make up our children.

THE ARROWHEAD: THE MIND

The arrowhead on an arrow belonging to a warrior was formed from the hardest possible material—flint, bone, or metal.[4] The arrowhead had to be sharpened. The sharper the point, the more deadly it became. A dull arrowhead would not have the same effect as one that had been sharpened.

When my husband and I got married, we registered for a cheap set of kitchen knives. We had the same set for fifteen years, but they were terrible. Cutting a chicken breast was my least favorite chore because those knives were so dull. But for our fifteenth anniversary my husband, Josh, bought me a very expensive, very sharp knife from Williams Sonoma, and now I look forward to cutting a chicken breast. I can't wait to unsheathe that beauty and slice through some chicken like it "ain't no thing." The sharper the knife, the more successful the chef. The sharper the arrow, the more successful the warrior.

If our children are like arrows, then their minds are the arrowheads, and it's our job as the warriors who wield them to sharpen their minds.

Many parents today are training their children to process everything through their feelings. "How did that make you *feel*?" is a question they ask their kids on a regular basis. But God's Word doesn't tell us to build our lives on what we're feeling; it tells us to build our lives on the Rock. Feelings change. The Word of God does not. Feelings are sinking sand. God's Word is a firm foundation.

Remember, the arrowhead has to be formed from the hardest possible material. Arrowheads shaped by unchecked emotions and unstable feelings are going to be dull and useless. But arrowheads shaped by the tried and true promises found in God's Word will be the kind of arrows mentioned in Jeremiah 50:9: "Their arrows shall be like those of an expert warrior; none shall return in vain" (NKJV).

Of course, our children have feelings and emotions, but we must teach them that the most important question is not "How did that make you feel?" but "What does God's Word say about this?"

Sharpening the arrowhead

One day my son, Gus, came home very angry and upset with a grumpy lunchroom monitor. She never smiled. She expected them to be quiet while they ate

73

lunch. She took away recess minutes and made them walk laps—the whole grade, not just the troublemakers. He was so frustrated with her!

I listened and sympathized and shared with him about a grumpy bus driver I used to have. Then I told him that even though he may not *feel* like it, he must be patient with the lunchroom monitor. I explained to him that when a person seems grumpy or rude, it's probably because that person is under some stress. I pointed out that he didn't know what the lunchroom monitor might be dealing with at home, and even though he may *feel* like talking about her with all the other kids at recess, believers don't act on our feelings—we act on God's Word. And God's Word says we are to put on compassion, kindness, gentleness, humility, and patience. The next morning we prayed for the teacher by name and for the patience needed to walk in love toward her.

It may seem like a small lesson, but it's these little lessons that prepare children for adulthood. When they *feel* like walking out on their marriage, they will remember we don't base our decisions on how we feel but on God's Word. When they don't *feel* like going to church, when they don't *feel* like finishing college, when they don't *feel* like forgiving, when they don't *feel* like doing the right thing, when they don't *feel* as if God is fair—they will remember that faith is not about what we *feel* but about what God's Word *says*.

Let your kids express their feelings and emotions, but always bring them back to God's Word. Be an intentional warrior, taking advantage of every opportunity to help your children renew their minds. I believe every time you talk with them about God's Word, you're sharpening their arrowheads. You're helping them step into their God-given destiny to be transformed into the image of Christ.

> And do not be conformed to this world [any longer with its superficial values and customs], but be transformed and progressively changed [as you mature spiritually] by the renewing of your mind [focusing on godly values and ethical attitudes], so that you may prove [for yourselves] what the will of God is, that which is good and acceptable and perfect [in His plan and purpose for you].
> —ROMANS 12:2, AMP

Arrows that are going to make a difference in this world have to be trained to think differently. Arrows that are going to test and prove that God's will for their lives is good, perfect, and pleasing have to be sharpened. I don't know about you, but that is what I want my kids to prove.

I don't care if they prove they are the best athletes or the best students. I don't care if they prove they have more Instagram followers than anyone else at their school. I don't care if they prove they are successful in business. The only thing I care about their proving is that God's will for their lives is good, pleasing, and perfect; and the only way they can prove that is if they are renewing their minds with God's Word.

What are you doing to sharpen your arrowheads today? I know life gets busy and nightly devotionals with the whole family seem impossible. Trust me, I understand. That's why I love the following verses from Deuteronomy:

> So commit yourselves wholeheartedly to these words of mine. Tie them to your hands and wear them on your forehead as reminders. Teach them to your children. Talk about them when you are at home and when you are on the road, when you are going to bed and when you are getting up. Write them on the doorposts of your house and on your gates.
> —DEUTERONOMY 11:18–20

I am a huge fan of this model of discipleship. It's discipleship on the go. It's discipleship woven into every part of our lives. It's not a once-a-week Bible study that everyone dreads—it's an ongoing, never-ending discussion that you can pick up at any time. There's not a day that goes by that we don't talk to our kids about Jesus. And we never plan it. It's all very organic. We weave Jesus into everything. He's the answer to every problem. He's the reason for every celebration. He's our world—which makes renewing our kids' minds with His Word a very natural part of our day.

If you want arrows that are sharp enough to make a difference, daily wash the world off them with the water of God's Word.

THE ARROW SHAFT: THE BODY

The next part of the arrow is the body or the shaft. The shaft of a warrior's arrow was long, narrow, straight, and typically made of wood or reed.[5] The body is the primary structural element of an arrow and the part of the arrow that the arrowhead is fastened to.

If our children are like arrows and their minds represent the arrowheads, then their physical bodies represent the arrow shaft. God gave our children bodies to live in—physical bodies that experience the world through the five senses of sight, smell, hearing, taste, and touch. A mind without a body can't do what it was renewed to do in the same way an arrowhead can't do what it was sharpened to do without the straight-and-narrow arrow shaft.

Our bodies serve a purpose, as Paul points out in his first letter to the Corinthians:

> Or didn't you realize that your body is a sacred place, the place of the Holy Spirit? Don't you see that you can't live however you please, squandering what God paid such a high price for? The physical part of you is not some piece of property belonging to the spiritual part of you. God owns the whole works. So let people see God in and through your body.
> —1 CORINTHIANS 6:19–20, MSG

I grew up singing a song based on this scripture passage that emphasized our being the temple of the Holy Spirit. The point of the passage—and the song—is that our bodies are not our own. They were bought by God, and they serve as a dwelling place for His Holy Spirit. And just as the physical temple was a place filled with praise, power, and glory, our bodies are to be filled with praise, power, and glory.

The same is true of our children's bodies. Kids must understand that their heads, shoulders, knees, and toes—and everything in between—belong to God and serve a purpose: to bring honor to their Creator.

Our feet should take us places that bring God glory. Our hands should reach out in a way that causes others to see Jesus in us. Our ears should listen to things that make the name of Jesus great. Our mouths should sing His praises and point people to the truth. Our eyes should be looking at things that are acceptable in the sight of God. Our bodies are the vehicles God is driving to accomplish His plans throughout the earth.

The body of an arrow must be straight and narrow. I've never seen an arrow with a loop in the middle. The arrow won't fly straight if the shaft isn't straight. In the same way, our kids won't fly straight if we aren't carving out straight paths for them. The Bible gives us this instruction:

> So take a new grip with your tired hands and strengthen your weak knees. *Mark out a straight path for your feet* so that those who are weak and lame will not fall but become strong.
> —HEBREWS 12:12–13, EMPHASIS ADDED

Our children are the weakest people in our homes. Sure, your thirteen-year-old son might be able to bench-press more than you, but that doesn't mean he is as strong as you are. You have more life experience, more

God experience. Your brain is more developed than his. You've been knocked on your backside more times than he has, and you've gotten pretty good at getting back up. You may have a very strong-willed child living under your roof, but even the strongest strong-willed child is weak when it comes to the schemes and strategies of the enemy. If we don't determine to take a new grip with our tired hands, strengthen our stances, and mark out a straight path for our feet—the weak will fall. Our kids will fall.

Notice the verse doesn't say mark a straight path for your *children's* feet. It says mark a straight path for *your* feet. If we put boundaries in place for ourselves and choose to honor God with our bodies, our kids will not fall but will become strong. What a promise!

Is what you are watching bringing glory to God? Are the words you speak honoring Jesus and others? Do you take proper care of your temple through exercise and healthy eating? If you don't care about honoring God with your body, why should your children? The goal for both you and your children is for your bodies to bring glory to God. When you meet this goal, you help the world around you experience God.

THE FEATHER: THE SPIRIT

The last piece of the arrow—the part that ties it all together—is the tail, or the feathers. In biblical times feathers from birds such as eagles, vultures, or sea fowl were attached to the body of an arrow to stabilize it while in flight and to help with accuracy.[6]

If the arrowhead represents our children's minds and the arrow body represents their physical bodies, the feathers represent their spirits. You are a triune being. You are, at your core, a spirit that possesses a mind and lives in a body. Your spirit is the real you—your true self, the part of you that was created in the image of God, who is also a spirit being. The same is true for your children. They are spirits that possess a mind and live in a body.

Second Corinthians 5:17 tells us that "anyone who belongs to Christ has become a new person." That means when your children invite Jesus to be the Lord and Savior of their lives, something magnificent takes place. They receive brand-new, born-again, perfect spirits. Their minds and their physical bodies remain the same, but their old spirits pass away, and as *The Message* translation declares, "a new life burgeons!" (v. 17). The moment a child believes in his heart and confesses with his mouth that Jesus is Lord—whether he's at Sunday school, summer camp, or in your living room—he is a new creation in Christ.

Sadly many children start a journey with God but don't know how to continue on it. They long to obey and follow after Him, but without the knowledge that their new, perfect spirits have total and complete access to their heavenly Father, they find themselves in a losing battle with their flesh. Their spirits cry out, "God resists a prideful attitude," but their flesh responds, "You're not prideful; you're just confident." Their spirits say, "Don't go there and don't do that," but their flesh says, "You only live once; go for it."

If our kids don't grasp the significance of having a brand-new spirit, they will be in a constant state of conflict with their flesh. And that is not God's plan. He didn't send His only Son to conquer sin and death once and for all to watch the very ones He gave His life for struggle to keep their sin nature in check.

Sometime in my early twenties I realized that although I had given my life to Christ at a young age and He had given me a new spirit, I had stopped letting my spirit lead the way. My flesh—my mind, will, and emotions—were calling the shots, and I was living a very selfish lifestyle, drifting further and further from God.

Out of desperation I turned to God. He wrapped me in His arms, and I began to see that although I was reading my Bible and going to church, my spirit—the most precious gift I had ever received—was being neglected. I repented and asked Jesus to fill me afresh—to infuse my spirit with His—and He did. His life-giving Spirit freed me! I was my true self, and my true self didn't want to live a selfish, sinful lifestyle. My true self wanted to do what I was created to do—bring glory to God.

The role of the Holy Spirit

Matthew 3:16 tells us that after Jesus was baptized in the Jordan River, as He was coming up out of the water, the Holy Spirit descended like a dove—a feathered animal—and settled on Him. Remember, feathers were attached to the body of an arrow to stabilize it while in flight and help promote accuracy. The Holy Spirit wants to come and rest on your children like a dove. He wants to stabilize them and help them accurately hit the target that God has for them every day. Jesus wants to infuse your children's born-again spirits with His Spirit. He wants to talk to them and lead them and show them what steps to take—and then empower them and embolden them to take those steps. But His hands are tied if our children do not understand the significance of their born-again spirits and the role the Holy Spirit plays in their lives.

God's Spirit joins with our spirit, Romans 8:16 tells us, and affirms that we are God's children. Therefore, we don't have to live a life controlled by our sinful nature. Our spirts can be led by the Spirit of God—and we couldn't ask for a more accurate and steady guide!

If we don't want our arrows to return in vain, we must parent them like the triune beings they are. We must sharpen their minds with God's Word, create straight paths for them to walk, and allow the Holy Spirit to lead them with accuracy. And we must trust God, "who makes everything holy and whole," according to 1 Thessalonians 5:23, to "put [our children] together—spirit, soul, and body" for we know that "the One who called [us] is completely dependable. If he said it, he'll do it!" (MSG).

QUESTIONS FOR DISCUSSION

1. Psalm 127 says that our children are gifts. Do your children feel more like burdens than gifts most of the time? If so, how can you break that cycle? If not, how have you been able to look past all the inconveniences of parenting to see that your children are gifts and treat them as such?

2. Our children are like arrows, and their minds are like arrowheads. We must sharpen our arrowheads with God's Word. Describe what discipleship looks like in your family. What are some ways you can be more intentional about exposing your kids to God's Word?

3. Hebrews 12:12-13 says we are to mark out a straight path for our feet so that those who are weak and lame will not fall but will become strong. Discuss why the paths parents walk could cause their children to either fall or become strong. Is your body bringing glory to God?

4. If our kids don't grasp the significance of having brand-new spirits, they will be in a constant state of conflict with their flesh. How can we help our kids be more aware of their spirits and the access they have to the very life of God within them?

5. Our kids are triune beings just as we are. Which part of them have you neglected the most? Which part of them have you nurtured the most? How can you adopt a more balanced approach to parenting your children?

Prayer for Parents

Lord, I thank You for my children. They are not burdens. They are gifts—perfect gifts from You. Help me to see them as You see them. When I feel inconvenienced, come and remind me of how blessed I am to be a parent. Forgive me for being ungrateful. Lord, thank You for showing me that my children are triune beings and that I have a responsibility to nurture and train their minds, bodies, and spirits. Help me to sharpen the minds of my children by renewing them with God's Word. May discipleship be natural and organic in our home. May You be the center of our focus and a frequent part of our conversations. We will weave You into everything. Lord, help me to mark out a straight path so that my children will be strong. Our bodies are Your temple, and we will see them as such. Our eyes, ears, mouth, hands, and feet will bring You glory. Awaken us daily to Your Spirit, which is alive in us. Help us to be aware and to be led by Your Spirit in all things. In Jesus' name, amen.

Confession for Children

I am a gift from God to my parents. I am an arrow. My spirit represents my true self. I have a mind and I live in a body. God's Spirit joins with my spirit to remind me of who I am and leads me into all truth. I renew my mind with the Word of God. My feelings change, but God's Word does not. I build my life on the Rock. My body is the temple of the Holy Spirit, and I will honor God with my body. My feet will take me places that bring God glory. My hands will reach out in a way that causes others to see Jesus in me. My ears will listen to things that make the name of Jesus great. My mouth will sing His praises and point people to the truth. My eyes will look at things that are acceptable in the sight of God. My body is the vehicle God is driving to accomplish His plans throughout the earth.

Chapter 6

OUR ROLE AS PARENTS

I N THE LAST chapter we considered Solomon's wisdom regarding children from Psalm 127:

> Children are a gift from the Lord; they are a reward from him. Children born to a young man are like arrows in a warrior's hands. How joyful is the man whose quiver is full of them! He will not be put to shame when he confronts his accusers at the city gates.
>
> —PSALM 127:3–6

He reminded us not only that our children are gifts from God but also that they are like arrows. We learned that these human arrows are made up of three parts—body, soul, and spirit—and that if we desire to help them accomplish their purposes, we have to nurture their whole being—all three parts.

Now let's place ourselves in this verse. If our children are like arrows, what does that make us? Solomon says "children...are like arrows in a *warrior's* hands" (v. 4, emphasis added).

That's right. You, my friend, are a warrior! The Hebrew word for *warrior* is *gibbowr*, which can also be translated "hunter," "soldier," "champion," "giant," "mighty man," or "mighty hero."[1] Would you use any of those words to describe yourself as a parent? If you answered, "Um, no, not even close," you're in good company. Gideon can identify.

Judges 6 tells us that after a long season of embarrassment, fruitless labor, scarcity, and being controlled by the Midianites, the children of Israel cried out to God and asked for help. God answered their cry and sent the angel of the Lord, which is believed to be Jesus, to notify one of the Israelites—Gideon—that he was going to be their deliverer. This account is one of my favorite "Oh, hey, just a heads up" moments in all of Scripture.

> Then the angel of the Lord came and sat beneath the great tree at Ophrah, which belonged to Joash of the clan of Abiezer. Gideon son of Joash was threshing wheat at the bottom of a winepress to hide the grain from the Midianites. The angel of the Lord appeared to him and said, "Mighty hero, the Lord is with you!"
>
> —JUDGES 6:11–12

Threshing wheat in Gideon's day was not an easy task. It was a process that required a great deal of effort. Typically wheat was threshed on a hilltop, so when a gentle breeze came along, it would blow away the chaff.[2]

But Gideon was working in the bottom of a winepress, hiding from the Midianites, who had been known to swoop in and steal the Israelites' wheat as soon as it was threshed. (See Judges 6:3–6, 11.) The angel appeared to Gideon right in the middle of a typical, strenuous, and humiliating work day.

As parents, the work we do can be tedious, exhausting, and sometimes very humiliating. There's nothing like getting a call from your child's principal informing you that he or she punched someone in the face at recess or was caught cheating on a test. It's difficult not to take our children's mistakes personally. I've had a few phone calls from the principal that left me feeling sick to my stomach and worried that because my child made a bad decision, every teacher at his school would hear about it and assume I was a horrible mother. The enemy so enjoys moments like that. He's the king of condemnation, and it's vital that we recognize his accusations so we can quickly shut him up.

WHO, ME?

Gideon was hidden from the Midianites, but he wasn't hidden from God. Jesus knew right where to find him, and He knew the exact words Gideon needed to hear: "Mighty hero, the Lord is with you!" (Judg. 6:12).

I'm sure he looked around in surprise, thinking, "Who, me?" in the same way you may have looked around and wondered when you read a few paragraphs ago that you are a warrior. The word Jesus used when he called Gideon "a mighty hero" is the same word Solomon used for "warrior" when he wrote, "Children born to a young man are like arrows in a warrior's hands" (Ps. 127:4). Gideon did not feel like a mighty hero, and you may not feel like a warrior; but remember, we don't base our lives on how we feel. We base our lives on what God's Word says, and God's Word says you are a warrior.

If you're struggling with that truth, I want you to know it's OK to ask questions. Gideon didn't immediately drop everything and run into battle when he heard the angel's words. Look at his response.

> "Sir," Gideon replied, "if the Lord is with us, why has all this happened to us? And where are all the miracles our ancestors told us about? Didn't they say, 'The Lord brought us up out of Egypt'? But now the Lord has abandoned us and handed us over to the Midianites."
>
> —JUDGES 6:13

Jesus wasn't offended by Gideon's questions or his doubt. He didn't head to another tree to find someone else who wouldn't ask questions. No, He told Gideon to go with the strength he had to rescue his people, and He reassured him that God was with him. Gideon responded with another question expressing his doubt.

"But, Lord," Gideon replied, "how can I rescue Israel? My clan is the weakest in the whole tribe of Manasseh, and I am the least in my entire family" (v. 15). The Lord easily countered Gideon's "but." He said to him, "I will be with you. And you will destroy the Midianites as if you were fighting against one man" (v. 16).

Gideon was still a bit unsure, so he asked God for a sign to prove that it was really the Lord who was speaking to him (vv. 17–18). After he got the sign, he went on to do exactly what he was sent to do—deliver God's people from the Midianites.

GOD'S STRENGTH IN YOUR WEAKNESS

You may have some "buts" for God with regard to your call to be a warrior parent, and that's OK. God can handle your questions.

"But God, how can I be a warrior parent when I didn't have godly parents growing up?" "But God, how can I be a warrior parent when my kid's dad isn't in the picture?" "But God, how can I be a warrior parent when I am a new believer?" "But God, how can I be a warrior parent when I'm so weak?"

Get honest with God. Go ahead. Lay out all your doubts for Him and allow Him to reassure you. Allow Him to convince you—not that you're the best parent ever but that He is with you on this parenting journey. Oh, if every parent could become thoroughly convinced that God is with him or her even on the typical, exhausting, and humiliating days!

When you get real with God, you give Him an invitation to prove His strength in your weakness. You surrender all your insufficiencies to His sufficiency. And He says the same thing to you that He spoke to Gideon: "Go in your might! And the Lord will go with you!" (See verse 14.)

Gideon was told to go in his might, but he didn't

think he had any might. Remember, he said his family was the weakest clan and he was the weakest in his family. (See verse 15.) The enemy would like to persuade you to believe that you don't have any might either, but that's not true. God has given you a spirit of power and commanded you to be strong in the Lord in the power of His might. (See 2 Timothy 1:7 and Ephesians 6:10.) *When you don't have any might to go in, borrow His!* He has an endless supply, and He has given you access to it!

You may not see yourself as a warrior parent, but that's how God sees you, and if you're going to be the hunter, soldier, champion, giant, mighty, heroic parent God has called you to be, you must start seeing yourself as He sees you. You are a warrior with an arrow in hand.

I'm concerned that if we don't get hold of this warrior revelation, our children will end up as decorative arrows that sit around collecting dust on a shelf instead of going out to fulfill their God-given purposes. A warrior doesn't sharpen an arrowhead, straighten the shaft, and adhere feathers to the tail of an arrow to keep it in his quiver. He has every intention of confidently releasing that arrow and watching it fly straight toward its intended target. And that's what we as parents are meant to do.

WHAT'S YOUR TARGET?

Many Christian parents have a goal of raising godly kids—ones who know Jesus and are led by His Spirit. But how many are aiming their arrows at a God-given target? How many have a sense of purpose in mind for their children? As a mighty warrior armed with a spiritual weapon, what are you aiming your arrows at? What target do you have your sights set on?

Some parents aim their children toward a great education. They send them off at an early age to learn their shapes, colors, letters, and numbers. They spend hours studying for the spelling bee with them. They reward them for good grades and punish them for bad grades. They devote much time and energy to making sure their kid has the best class projects. Their bull's-eye? Seeing their children graduate from college.

Some parents aim their children toward sports. They sign them up for little league as soon as they are of age. They spend hours up at the batting cages. They pay for private lessons. Their kid's greatness is determined by how he or she performed at the last game. They miss church on weekends for tournaments. The bull's-eye for their children is seeing them compete at the college or professional level.

Some parents aim their children toward excellent behavior. They teach them to say "yes, ma'am" and "no, ma'am." They make sure they know how to shake a person's hand and look the person in the eye. They make sure they never cut in line or say a bad word. They reward them when they complete all their chores and punish them when they don't. The bull's-eye for their children is seeing them become good, responsible people.

Some parents aim their children toward financial success. They teach them the value of a dollar. They make their kids earn everything because nothing in life is free. They set an example by working all the time and justify it by saying they are good providers. The bull's-eye for their children is for the kids to get a job at which they earn lots of money.

Some parents aim their children toward nothing. They have no vision for their kids, no bull's-eye whatsoever.

Please hear me: *The bull's-eye you're aiming your kids at will determine what they believe their purpose to be.* You may not ever sit them down and tell them the reason they exist is to get a great job and make lots of money, but if that's the direction you're aiming them in, that is what they are going to believe.

It's heartbreaking to think about the people I went to high school with who were aimed at the wrong targets. I had a friend whose world revolved around sports and who was talented enough to receive an athletic scholarship—only to suffer a career-ending injury in college. Just like that, his target suddenly vanished, and he was left flying aimlessly through life. He had no idea who he was or why he was here. Sports was filling the God-sized hole in his heart, and when sports were no longer an option, he turned to drugs, ended up in rehab, and landed in a casket at twenty-three years old. Yes, you read that right: twenty-three.

Don't misunderstand. Getting a good education, participating in sports, exhibiting exemplary behavior, and learning to properly handle money are not bad pursuits. But if they are the primary targets you are aiming your kids at, you have chosen the wrong bull's-eye. How do I know? Search the scriptures. You'll be hard pressed to find any about the importance of focusing on these or other goals parents typically have for their kids. We need to readjust our sights. *We need to get focused on God's purpose for our children.*

RAISING A GENERATION WITH PURPOSE

The number of Christian adults I run into who are unaware of their purpose amazes me. They have read all the books on the subject, listened to all the podcasts, and taken all the gifts assessment tests; yet they still don't know why they are here. I believe this plague of purposelessness is due to the fact that parents are waiting too long to start instilling God-given destiny in their children. When the children grow up, they are just as clueless about God's plan for them as they were when they were young.

Perhaps this is one reason Rick Warren's *The Purpose Driven Life* is among the best-selling Christian books of all time. Every person, deep down, desires to know the answer to the age-old question, "What is my purpose?" And because a generation of parents never answered that question, when their children see a book with the subtitle "What on Earth Am I Here For?" they are going to pick it up in the hope of finding the answer they've been seeking.

I'm thankful for Pastor Rick and the countless people he has helped to discover their God-given purpose. But parents, let's not raise a generation of kids who are clueless about why they exist, hoping they figure it out when they get old enough to purchase a book that will help them discover it. *Let's raise a generation of kids who know their purpose from a young age!* Let's raise a generation of kids who not only know their purpose but are walking in it before they head off to college. Let's raise a generation of kids who are so in tune with God's purpose for their *own* lives that they can help others discover *their* God-given mission.

It's startling to consider how little time parents spend talking purpose with their children. Tom Kersting, author and family counselor, says the average American parents spend just 3.5 minutes in meaningful conversation with their child per week.[3] Not per day, guys—per *week*! Let's not be average American parents, because average American parents are failing miserably.

We can't release arrows that do what they were fashioned to do if we spend no more than thirty seconds a day talking to them about meaningful things. That statistic makes my entire body burn with holy discontent.

It's time to wake up, parents! It's time to put the electronic devices down. It's time to stop making excuses. It's time to stop depending on the church to reveal our kids' purposes. It's time to stop cramming our schedules so full that we don't have time for what matters. It's time to find a healthy balance so our jobs don't leave our kids fatherless or motherless the majority of the week. It's time to turn off the TV. It's time to stop trying to improve ourselves all the time and start doing something to impact the next generation. It's time to stop being selfish.

I know this opinion may sound harsh, but in my view, a parent who spends less than thirty seconds a day engaged in meaningful conversation with their children is incredibly selfish. We need to realize that Paul's admonition to the Philippians applies equally well to us: "Don't be selfish; don't try to impress others. Be humble, thinking of others as better than yourselves. Don't look out only for your own interests, but take an interest in others, too" (2:3–4).

We busy ourselves trying to impress others with our clean houses, our big bank accounts, the number of church functions we attend, our awe-inspiring Instagram accounts, and the number of activities we juggle. Paul says don't. Just don't. Don't try to impress others. Stop it! Instead, take an interest in others. *Take an interest in your children.*

It's time to start talking to them. It's time to start investing in them. It's time to start making the most of meaningful moments with them.

But how?

First, we must pray for meaningful moments. Every day, ask God for a discipleship moment with your children. Ask Him to help you to be sensitive to His still, small voice. Ask Him to help you know the right words to say. Ask Him to soften your children's hearts so the seeds you plant in them don't get snatched up but take root and produce fruit!

Declare Matthew 13:8–9 over your children, which I paraphrase here from multiple translations: "My children's hearts are good, rich soil. The seed of God's Word that I speak falls on their good, rich soil and continues to produce a harvest—thirty-, sixty-, and one-hundred-fold. My children have ears to hear. Let them listen, consider, and comprehend what I am saying. The seeds I sow will produce a harvest beyond my wildest dreams."

Second, we must take advantage of every opportunity. My favorite place to have meaningful conversations with my kids is in the car. And their favorite place to have meaningful conversations is in their rooms, right before bedtime. They will do anything to get out of going to bed on time, including opening their hearts and engaging in a great conversation. Even though I am tired and ready to clock out of mom-duty for the day, if I feel the Holy Spirit prompting me to wait before I turn off the lights, I wait. Everything in me wants to flip the switch and say, "We'll talk tomorrow. It's bedtime," but every time I've taken an interest in my kids instead of in the whirlpool bath that is calling my name, God has shown up!

Third, we must know what their purpose is. A wise person once said, "The two most important days in your life are the day you are born and the day you find out why."[4] That statement is pure gold. If we want to instill purpose in our kids through meaningful conversation, we have to know and understand what their God-given purpose is. And that's what we are going to discover next!

What I'm about to say may sound daunting, but I'm going to leave you with the same words Jesus spoke to Gideon: "I will be with you. And you will destroy the Midianites as if you were fighting against one man" (Judg. 6:16).

Warrior parent, you can do this. The Lord is with you. Go in His might! It will be easier than you think because God is with you. You'll face opposition, but it will be as if you're fighting against only one man. Gideon and his one-hundred-man army took down 135,000 Midianites. All they had to do was raise a torch and give a victory shout, and the Lord took care of the rest.

> It was just after midnight, after the changing of the guard, when Gideon and the 100 men with him reached the edge of the Midianite camp. Suddenly, they blew the rams' horns and broke their clay jars. Then all three groups blew their horns and broke their jars. They held the blazing torches in their left hands and the horns in their right hands, and they all shouted, "A sword for the Lord and for Gideon!" Each man stood at his position around the camp and watched as all the Midianites rushed around in a panic, shouting as they ran to escape. When the 300 Israelites blew their rams' horns, the Lord caused the warriors in the camp to fight against each other with their swords.
>
> —JUDGES 7:19–22

Can you see the enemy rushing around in a panic as you start to believe that your children are like arrows in the hand of a mighty warrior and that *you* are that warrior? Pick up your bow and get ready!

QUESTIONS FOR DISCUSSION

1. What one word would you use to describe your parenting mind-set?

2. Gideon had several questions for God about being a mighty warrior. What questions do you have for God about being a warrior parent?

3. Do you think your parents had a target in mind for you as they raised you? Looking back, what would you say their bull's-eye for your life was? How has that affected your adulthood?

4. What have you been aiming your children at? What is your primary goal for their lives?

5. In what areas of your life have you been selfish and neglected to take an interest in your children? What is the Holy Spirit leading you to change so you can begin having more meaningful moments with your children?

PRAYER FOR PARENTS

Lord, I want to see myself the way You see me. I am a warrior parent. I am a hunter, a soldier, a champion, a giant, a mighty parent, and a mighty hero. I know You have called me to go in the power of Your might. If I am going to raise children who make an impact in this world, I know I have to be wholly dependent on Your strength. Help me to rise up and boldly release the arrows You have placed in my hand. Help me to set my sights on what You have for my children. Instill in me everything I need to raise children who know their purpose and are confidently walking in it. Lord, forgive me for being selfish. I will no longer live trying to impress others. I commit myself to taking an interest in my children. I ask You for opportunities to engage in meaningful conversation with them. Keep me focused on what's important. Steady my aim. In Jesus' name, amen.

CONFESSION FOR CHILDREN

I am an arrow, designed for a purpose. My parents are warrior parents. God has placed them in my life for a reason. I trust that they will be used by God to aim me in the right direction. My heart is good, fertile soil. When my parents sow God's Word into me, the seed will take root and produce a healthy harvest. I don't allow distractions to steal the seed from my heart. I have ears to hear. And I will use my ears to listen to my parents. They aren't wasting their breath when they talk to me. I exist for a reason, a reason that goes way beyond sports, school, friends, and being a good person. I will fulfill my God-given purpose.

Chapter 7

SALT OF THE EARTH

THE CULTURE WE live in loves to point fingers—always looking for someone to blame for why the world is the way it is. I was shocked to learn that many people blame Mister Rogers of the children's television series *Mister Rogers' Neighborhood* for the "everyone is special" mentality that has been adopted in schools and sports teams all over our country. Fred Rogers wanted kids to feel valued and loved simply for being who they were. He was constantly reminding his little viewers, "You never have to do anything sensational for people to love you."[1] Your worth, in other words, is not based on how great you are at sports or academics. You are special just because you're you.

How could this mentality hurt society? It seems that many millennials—adults born between 1980 and 1995—who grew up regularly hearing they were special and who collected scores of "participation trophies" for playing on sports teams where there were no winners or losers are struggling to succeed in the real world. I'm sure you've seen comments on social media from millennials referring to the fact that "adulting is hard." Is it possible that being an adult is difficult for this generation because after they leave home and enter the real world, they soon discover they aren't as special as they thought they were?

They don't get a job just because they show up for an interview; they must have qualifications to offer an employer. They don't get paid at a job just for sitting at a desk; they must actually do something worthwhile or risk getting fired. Their worth is no longer based on their being "special"; their worth is based on their performance. Don't perform, don't get a paycheck. And if the person across the hall is smarter, more driven, and more talented, that person will be the one who is treated as special.

Now is this really all Mister Rogers' fault? Should we be pointing fingers at the gentle soul who was actually sharing the heart of God with millions of impressionable young people week in and week out in his cardigan and sneakers? I don't think so. The people to blame are the parents who didn't teach their kids *why* they are special—and the responsibility that comes with being so.

WHY WE ARE SPECIAL

The gospel is based on Jesus' perfect love for us—a love that we don't have to earn. It's a love that says, "You are special to Me not because of what you can *do* for Me but because of who you *are* to Me." And it's a gift He offers to us freely.

> God saved you by his grace when you believed.
> And you can't take credit for this; it is a gift
> from God. Salvation is not a reward for the good
> things we have done, so none of us can boast
> about it. For we are God's masterpiece. He has
> created us anew in Christ Jesus, so we can do
> the good things he planned for us long ago.
> —EPHESIANS 2:8–10

You don't have to do anything sensational for God
to love you. He loves you because you are special to
Him. Psalm 139 says that every single moment, God is
thinking of you and cherishing you in every thought.
His desires toward you are more numerous than the
grains of sand on every shore. I could list scripture
after scripture proving that you are special to God
and have been since before you took your first breath.

Now the world may tell you a different story; the
world may say you're a dime a dozen. And that's
why the millennial generation is confused. They've
believed the lie that they are special to *everyone*. But
not everyone loves them based on who they are. Not
everyone thinks of them every moment of the day. Not
everyone believes they are a masterpiece. God's Word
says that God does; but sadly, they are determined to
convince everyone else to have the same view.

The problem is that trying to convince the world
you are special is futile. Living convinced that God
says you are special, however, is fruitful. If you want
your children to believe they are special, *you* must
first believe they are special—not in the "everyone gets

a trophy" way but in the "God knows me intimately, cares about me personally, and has a unique plan for me to walk in" way.

As we learned in chapter 2, Moses' mother, Jochebed, saw that her son was special. It was the reason she did what she could to ensure that the Egyptians didn't kill him. "She saw that he was a special baby and kept him hidden for three months" (Exod. 2:2). Moses was special not because he had done anything sensational—at this point, all he could do was cry, nurse, sleep, and dirty a diaper. He was special because God loved him.

Don't be afraid to tell your children they are special. They need to grow up hearing those words. They need to understand from an early age that God says they are His masterpiece, not because of what they look like or what they do but because of who they are—a son or daughter of God. And because they are special, God has a special assignment for them. I believe Moses grew up with the affirmation that he was special, created *on* purpose *for* a purpose, and when it was time to step into that purpose, he was ready.

KIDS ON A MISSION

Your kids can be ready too. But they don't have to wait till they are forty years old, as Moses was when God called him. Ephesians 2:10 tells us, "For we are God's masterpiece. He has created us anew in Christ Jesus, so *we can do the good things he planned for us long ago*" (emphasis added). *The Message Bible* says it like this: "He creates each of us by Christ Jesus to join him in the work he does, the good work he has gotten ready for us to do, work we had better be doing" (v. 10).

God is a master planner, and He has good assignments planned for His little masterpieces—those arrows in your hand. If your children have been born again, you can begin sending them on their missions. There is no need to wait until they are eighteen or twenty-one. If you do, they will miss out on so many opportunities to experience God's working in and through them! And they may become distracted and consumed with trying to *feel* special instead of focusing on the assignments God has prepared for them because they already *are* special.

So what is their mission? What are the good works God has prepared for them? What target are we to aim our arrows at? When I started asking the Holy Spirit those questions, He gave me three words: salt, light, love.

Our children are not here to take up space and consume resources until they are "old enough" to make a difference. The purpose of our sending them to school should not be solely to educate them. Sure, we want them to learn how to read, write, and do arithmetic. Bonus points if they figure out how to successfully climb a rope, make some friends, and win a class party for collecting the most box tops.

But what if our kids have a higher purpose? What if school is more than test scores and learning how to multiply fractions? What would our nation look like if every classroom had a handful of kids on the roll who understood their God-given purpose and were being encouraged to walk in it daily? Wherever God has planted your children—their neighborhood, home-school co-op, sports league, art class, church, or glee club—He has called them to be salt, light, and love.

TEACH YOUR KIDS TO BE SALTY

Let's talk salt. Matthew 5:13 says, "You are the salt of the earth. But what good is salt if it has lost its flavor? Can you make it salty again? It will be thrown out and trampled underfoot as worthless."

At a time when identity is being threatened as never before, we need to be sure our children understand who they are and why they are here. Jesus lays it out pretty clearly. He declares, "You are the salt of the earth" (v. 13). We need to insert our children's places of influence into Matthew 5:13. I tell my kids all the time, "You are the salt of your elementary school. You are the salt of Miss Jones' class." I do this because I know if they can grasp this truth and recognize how valuable salt is, they'll never have to battle insignificance.

To unlock divine purpose in your children, you must teach them to be salty. And if you want to teach them to be salty, you must understand the properties of salt.

Salt is precious. I'm sure you've heard the expression "worth one's salt." It means "to be worth one's pay."[2] The word *salary* comes from the Latin *salarium* (*sal* is the Latin word for "salt"). Scholars don't agree on the origin of the word *salarium*, but most believe that it referred to the money given to Roman soldiers for the purchase of salt.[3] I don't have to tell you that your salary is valuable. You need your salary to pay your mortgage, buy groceries, clothe your family—essentially, to survive. Salt was as valuable to the Romans as your salary is to you.

We live in a day and age in which we are told to cut back on salt due to the overabundance we ingest, particularly in processed foods—which weren't available in biblical times—but that was not the case for those listening to the Sermon on the Mount. Roman soldiers were working, sweating, and losing salt all day long, so they needed this precious commodity for basic survival.

Ask any doctor: the human body can't live without salt, or sodium chloride, as a chemist would describe it. According to the Harvard Heart Letter of the Harvard Medical School, sodium is required "to transmit nerve impulses, contract and relax muscle fibers (including those in the heart and blood vessels), and maintain a proper fluid balance."[4]

Our nerve impulses send messages from our brains to our bodies—the kinds of messages, for example, that cause us to swerve out of the way when a car heading in our direction crosses over the center line. Salt makes our quick responses possible. And in the same way salt helps our bodies react properly to whatever may be happening around us, God can help your children react properly to whatever might be happening around them. Temptation, fear, rebellion—anything the enemy throws at them they will be able to swerve around, and as they swerve they will not only protect their purpose but also positively influence those around them.

When our muscles, including the heart, contract and relax, they get stronger. Salt makes that possible. As the salt of the earth we must contract and relax our faith muscle in order to have a positive impact in the world.

The greatest way to work our faith muscle is through prayer. If you want your children to make a difference, teach them to pray, particularly for people in their social circles. Have them ask the Holy Spirit to show them one person to pray for each day. It could be a classmate, a teacher, a bully, or a sibling. And then have them pray for that person before breakfast, on the way to school, or at bedtime. Every time they open their mouth to talk to a God they can't see and choose to trust that He hears them even though they might not receive an immediate answer, that relaxed faith muscle contracts and grows stronger. "Salty" people in the Spirit are people of prayer!

When our fluid balance is thrown off, we may become dehydrated, which can negatively affect cardiac and renal functions. Salt makes it possible for us to maintain proper fluid balance.[5] As the salt of the earth, we must quench the world's spiritual thirst. All over the world people are spiritually dehydrated. The human body usually can't survive more than three days without water;[6] what about the human spirit?

Jesus said that we have rivers of living water flowing from within us. That living water has salt in it, needed electrolytes to revive the weary. We're called to be like a cool sports drink that boosts the performance and sustains the energy of those running the race alongside us and to bring new life to the spiritually dead. Talk to your children about how God can use their smile, their words, and anything else they are willing to make available to Him to refresh someone who needs a drink of Jesus.

Salt is precious. You and your children are precious as well.

Salt preserves. It is difficult to imagine a world without refrigerators because we are so accustomed to walking into our kitchens and opening the doors to our temperature-controlled, well-lit, compartmentalized fridges filled with food that stays fresh for days. But there was a time when refrigerators didn't exist and food had to be preserved in other ways. In biblical times salt was used for this purpose. The reason salt works well as a preservative is that it draws moisture out of food—which decreases the bacteria that cause food to rot.

If we are the salt of the earth, we are called to act as a preservative. We are called to prevent God's standards from rotting away. We are called to keep the Bible fresh and desirable. We are on a mission to preserve the truth. It's essential for our children to recognize that without Christ-followers like them, standing for what's right and living according to the Word of God, God's presence in their places of influence will decay.

When we pull our families out of this world, we remove the preserving agents God has set in place.

Everything may be great at your house, but don't get so comfortable in your safe little bubble that you become callous to the rotting world around you. The morals and values of our country are spoiling. They're decaying, and as the salt of the earth, you and your children have a responsibility to preserve.

Have you washed your hands of that responsibility, failing to walk in your God-given identity and teach your children to walk in theirs? Are you apathetic? Do you find yourself thinking, "What's the point? This world is too far gone. It's too rotten, and nothing I do can stop the deterioration"? That's precisely how the prophet Jonah felt when God asked him to go to Nineveh. It took his being tossed into a salty ocean and being swallowed by a giant fish to realize that God could use one man to preserve an entire city.

May our kids be the salt that preserves God's plan for purity. May our kids be the salt that preserves God's plan for community. May our kids be the salt that preserves the fruit of the Spirit—"love, joy, peace, patience, kindness, goodness, faithfulness, gentleness, and self-control" (Gal. 5:22–23). May our kids be the salt that preserves faith and hope in a world where faith and hope are fading fast. The world is ever-changing, but may our kids be the salt that keeps God's way of doing things from passing away.

Salt adds flavor. You don't have to be a culinary genius to know that salt adds essential flavor to our food. Salt can "intensify aromas, balance other flavors, [and] make meat taste juicer."[7] In fact, as Kimberly Masibay points out, "salt makes pretty much everything taste better. Thanks to its chemical nature, salt has the amazing ability to intensify agreeable tastes and diminish disagreeable ones."[8] How does this work? Cooking gurus say salt "enhances foods by essentially turning up the volume of their salty flavors. Salt can also dial down the taste of bitter foods by suppressing our perception of bitterness, and balance other tastes like sweet and sour."[9] When a small amount of salt is added to a dish, "suddenly, our taste receptors can detect flavors they weren't able to sense before."[10] Salt is not added to food to make it taste salty but to make it taste the way it should. For instance, we add salt to our chocolate chip cookie dough not so our cookies taste salty but because salt intensifies the body's ability to taste the sweetness of the sugar.[11]

If we are the salt of the earth, we are called to intensify the God-flavors in this world while dialing down those that don't complement God's Word. Our kids should start every day thinking about how they have the ability, through their words and actions, to give people a taste of the goodness of God. They get to be like the sample-servers at Sam's Club—except instead of offering food, they are tasked to give out little samples of the fruit of the Spirit: love, joy, peace, patience, kindness, goodness, faithfulness, gentleness, and self-control. It's a win-win. Your children fulfill their purpose and their friends, teachers, and even their enemies get a taste of God's goodness that whets their appetites for more of Jesus.

Many believers today are living a "La Croix" brand of Christianity. If you have ever had a can of the trendy sparkling water, you know flavor isn't its best quality. We keep the office fridge stocked with La Croix, and people either love it or hate it. The memes suggesting what the different flavors should really be named always make me laugh. "Hint of hint of lime." "Shy watermelon." "Transported in a truck near bananas." "Previous tenant squeezed a lemon." Funny but true! If you blindfolded me, gave me a can of La Croix, and asked me to identify the flavor, I don't think I could do it. The flavors don't pop, because La Croix has zero sodium. That's right: no salt.

I don't want to live a La Croix brand of Christianity. I don't want the world around me to have a difficult time identifying the God-flavors in my life. I don't want to be a "hint of hint of hope"; I want to be hopeful! I don't want to be "shy gospel"; I want to be bold, as Peter was after he was filled with the Holy Spirit. I don't want to be "transported in a truck *near* the Holy Spirit"; I want to transport people into new levels of freedom because the Spirit of the Lord is upon me! I don't want to be "previous tenant squeezed the fruit of the Spirit"; I want the fruit of the Spirit to be intensified in my life so everyone I come in contact with can taste those agreeable God-flavors produced when we abide in Him! Let's bring out the God-flavors. God desires this for every one of His children, including the ones He's loaned you!

Salt balances flavors. As mentioned before, this amazing additive has the ability to enhance agreeable tastes and minimize disagreeable ones,[12] maintaining a balance that helps us to better enjoy the food we

113

eat. As Christians we must help to bring a similar but spiritual balance to our spheres of influence. Some Christians are so focused on God's grace that they forget about His truth; and some are so focused on God's truth that they forget about His grace. Jesus was focused on *both* grace and truth. He balanced the flavors of grace and truth beautifully—and it's our destiny to do the same.

We can be super friendly to a sinner for his entire life, but if we never share the truths found in God's Word with him, he will continue to walk in darkness and end up separated from God for eternity. On the other hand, we'll never reach a sinner by beating him over the head with scripture. We won't even get our foot in the door to share God's truth without first extending love and grace. *We are called to balance the flavors of truth and grace.*

Our children must understand that if they want to help people taste and see that the Lord is good, they must master the art of sharing God's truth in love. They will need an example of how to do this. They will need to see it lived out in front of them. And they are looking to you, Mighty Warrior. Show them how it's done.

Before your children leave the nest, you'll have ample opportunity to share God's truth in love with them. When they fall, you'll be there, ready to pick them up, extend grace, and remind them what the truth of God's Word says. You'll be able to help dial down the bitterness that disappointment and failures bring while intensifying the flavors their souls crave.

Salt is precious. Salt preserves. Salt adds flavor. Salt brings balance.

Sit down with your children, show them where in their Bibles Jesus is recorded as saying that they are the salt of the earth, and talk about things they can do, starting now, to begin living a "salty" life!

QUESTIONS FOR DISCUSSION

1. What are your thoughts on the "everyone is special" mentality? Do you tell your kids they are special often? If you were to ask them to tell you why they are special, what do you think their answer might be?

2. Have you been waiting until your children are "old enough" to send them on mission? Why do you think our society belittles the effect that children can have in their places of influence?

3. Discuss some of the godly values you have seen decay in this world during your lifetime. Share your thoughts on the personal responsibility you have to be a preserving agent. How can you communicate this personal responsibility to your children?

4. Jesus was 100 percent grace and 100 percent truth. Salt helps balance flavors. How can you balance truth and grace and teach your children to do the same?

5. Salt intensifies flavor. Which God-flavors are the most difficult to detect in your life? Which God-flavors are the easiest to identify in your life? Discuss the God-flavors you see your children producing. How do you plan to focus them on being who Jesus says they are—the salt of the earth?

Prayer for Parents

Lord, thank You for reminding me of how special I am to You—not because I have done anything sensational but because Jesus did something sensational. I am special because I am a child of God. My children are special because they are children of God. Thank You for choosing us. You have special assignments for us—not so that we can hopefully become special someday, *but because You have already made us special. Help me to fulfill my purpose. Help me to be the salt of the earth. Help me to intensify God-flavors and diminish flavors that are not agreeable to Your Word. Help me to see myself as a preserving agent—someone who is called to make sure Your way of doing things does not pass away. I want people to line up and say they have tasted and seen that God is good through my life. I pray that as I commit to being the salt of the earth, my children will imitate me, and we will begin to walk on mission together! In Jesus' name, amen.*

Confession for Children

I am special—not because of anything I've done but because of what Jesus did for me. I am a child of God. He is always thinking precious thoughts about me. He calls me His masterpiece. He has given me a special mission because I am special to Him. Jesus said that I am the salt of the earth. Everywhere I go I help people taste and see that the Lord is good. I am called to make sure God's way of doing things does not pass away. I will stand for purity, community, faith, hope, and love. I understand that I am on a mission to preserve truth. My life brings out the satisfying, God-flavors in life. I balance the flavors of truth and grace. The way I live intensifies the ability of everyone around me to taste the sweetness of God.

Chapter 8

LIGHT OF THE WORLD

F EARLESS PARENTS UNDERSTAND that their children are here for a reason—to be salt, light, and love. Hopefully you're now more aware than ever of your responsibility to be the salt of the earth, and you're excited about releasing your arrows to preserve and flavor their worlds with the truth of God's Word as well.

Now let's consider the second aspect of both our purpose and our children's. Jesus told us in His Sermon on the Mount what it is:

> You are the light of the world—like a city on a hilltop that cannot be hidden. No one lights a lamp and then puts it under a basket. Instead, a lamp is placed on a stand, where it gives light to everyone in the house. In the same way, let your good deeds shine out for all to see, so that everyone will praise your heavenly Father.
>
> —MATTHEW 5:14–16

We are not only the salt of the earth but also the light of the world. These are not things we *do* but who we *are*—and not just some of the time. We are salt. We are light. If you don't feel very salty or can't see yourself as a city on a hilltop that cannot be hidden, you may be having an identity crisis: a "personal psychosocial conflict especially in adolescence that involves confusion about one's social role and often a sense of loss of continuity to one's personality."[1]

It's interesting but not surprising to me that identity crises begin especially in adolescence. Our children must understand their role in God's kingdom from a young age. We must continually remind them that God has called them to be salt, light, and love while helping them hold on to their God-given personalities.

DIFFERENT PERSONALITIES, SAME PURPOSE

My kids all have very different personalities. My oldest is a very driven, very competitive rule-follower. He has a lot of me in him. He likes to achieve and accomplish goals. He loves to study and learn new things. He is very comfortable with familiar friends, but it takes him a while to warm up to new peers. You can tell what he's thinking just by observing his body language. He thrives with routine. He wants to know the entire plan for the day before the day begins and struggles if the plan changes. He enjoys conversation and is excellent at sharing detail.

My middle child is a lot like her dad. She doesn't

care much for routine—each day is a new day, and she'll figure it out as she goes. She is free-spirited. She loves to create and explore. While my other two would be happy watching a movie they have already seen ten times, she wants to see something she's never seen before. She is extremely loyal and doesn't make many new friends but loves the friends she does have deeply. Her love language is definitely gifts. She enjoys giving gifts, and if I want to make her day, I bring her home a special treat from the grocery store—even something as small as a pencil—and she feels appreciated and loved. She has a tender heart and is quick to forgive or ask for forgiveness.

The baby of the family is her own unique little gal. She is extremely social—more social than her dad and I combined. She loves people. She adores her teachers at school and church. She makes her babysitters feel as if they are the greatest humans on earth. She gets to know a new friend every day at school. Unlike her two older siblings, who still prefer for Mom to lay out their outfits each day, she wants to pick out her clothes. She enjoys to-do lists and chore charts. She is not afraid to take on new challenges.

I'm sure as you read this you're thinking about how different your kids are from each other or how different you are from your siblings. We're all different, but we all have the same purpose, our children included. We are called to be light. How your oldest carries out that calling will look different from how your youngest carries it out—and that's a good thing! Our differences showcase the beauty of God's creation.

The goal when aiming your children toward their God-given purposes is not to have them act, talk, and process things in an identical way; the goal is to have children who treasure their God-given personalities and allow God to shine His light through them in unique ways. If we can raise a generation confident of their role in society while also keeping their personalities intact, we can put an end to the identity crisis that is affecting so many of our young people.

GOD AFFIRMS, SUSTAINS, AND SEPARATES THE LIGHT

Now, let's talk about light.

The first recorded spoken words of God are "Let there be light" (Gen. 1:3). And light was. Light existed even before God created the sun and the moon, so we know that light is more than a physical substance—it is also supernatural. Before the supernatural light came into existence, the earth was in a state of chaos. *The Message* describes it like this: "Earth was a soup of nothingness, a bottomless emptiness, an inky blackness" (vv. 1–2).

After God spoke light into existence, He "saw that the light was good (pleasing, useful) and He *affirmed* and *sustained* it; and God *separated* the light [distinguishing it] from the darkness" (Gen. 1:4, AMP, emphasis added).

I want you to notice three things that God did concerning the light. He affirmed it, He sustained it, and He separated it. That's a beautiful picture of our life in

Christ. We are the light of the world, and God affirms us, sustains us, and separates us from the darkness. God's Word confirms this truth.

Second Corinthians 1:21–22 declares that He affirms us: "God *affirms* us, making us a sure thing in Christ, putting his Yes within us. By his Spirit he has stamped us with his eternal pledge—a sure beginning of what he is destined to complete" (MSG, emphasis added).

First Corinthians 1:7–8 says that He sustains us: "...you are not lacking in any gift, as you wait for the revealing of our Lord Jesus Christ, who will *sustain* you to the end, guiltless in the day of our Lord Jesus Christ" (ESV, emphasis added).

And 1 Peter 2:9 makes it clear that He has separated us: "But you are a chosen people, *set aside* to be a royal order of priests, a holy nation, God's own; so that you may proclaim the wondrous acts of the One who called you out of inky darkness into shimmering light" (THE VOICE, emphasis added).

The fact that God affirms us is significant. If we want our light to shine, we must allow Him to be the source of our affirmation. If we look instead to people for love, approval, and acceptance, our light will grow dim.

We must also look to God as our sustainer, trusting Him with every area of our lives. We must fully surrender all to Him—withholding nothing—believing He will meet all our needs according to His riches in glory. If we look instead to our employer, our popularity, or our work ethic to sustain us, our light will grow dim.

Perhaps the most critical aspect of being the light of

the world is acknowledging that God has set us aside. He has called us out of the inky darkness and into the shimmering light. He has distinguished us—separated us—but so often we mix right back in with the darkness around us. *We can't be light if we're imitating darkness.* If we're becoming like the world instead of being transformed into the image of Jesus, we won't reach those God has called us to reach.

IN THE WORLD, BUT NOT OF IT

Does the fact that God has set us apart and called us out of darkness mean that we can't be a part of society? Should we get serious about finding another planet that could support human life and do our best to keep out any unsaved, worldly folk—along with R-rated movies, gangster rap, drugs, and alcohol? Is God calling us to create a perfect Christian universe?

No, not at all. We are called to be *in* the world, but not *of* it. Because many Christian parents don't understand what it means to be set apart to Christ while remaining in the world, they try to keep their children far away from ungodly people and influences. As a result, these children never interact with the world and have no opportunities to shine their light.

That's not the model Jesus set before us! Jesus declared that He is the Light of the world (see John 8:12; 9:5), and He did not hide Himself away, afraid the darkness of the day would corrupt Him.

Think about it: If anyone had reason to hide from the world, it was Jesus. He had to live a perfect life for the cross to be effective. Wouldn't you have been tempted to hide away in the mountains, away from everyone and everything, so you would be less tempted to sin? I mean, the salvation of the world was hinging on His ability to remain sinless! Let's not chance it, right?

But Jesus didn't hole up and hide out. He did not cover His light under a bushel or a basket. No, He let His light shine without becoming like the world. He was in the world, a friend of sinners, but not of the world. As author and theologian Kevin DeYoung points out, Jesus didn't condone sin or participate in it, but He accepted those who received Him and His message:

> Jesus was a friend of sinners not because he winked at sin, ignored sin, or enjoyed light-hearted revelry with those engaged in immorality. Jesus was a friend of sinners in that he came to save sinners and was very pleased to welcome sinners who were open to the gospel, sorry for their sins, and on their way to putting their faith in Him.[2]

What a model for our young people! We must teach them to welcome sinners who are open to the gospel, sorry for their sins, and on their way to putting their faith in Jesus. Because that was the criteria for Jesus' interaction with the world, it should be ours and our children's as well.

Jesus never did anything without purpose. Every step He took was intentional. Every meal He sat down to had a goal beyond mere sustenance. But His mission called Him to be in the world, letting His light shine in a way that would transform people from the inside out. And He fulfilled this mission without compromise, as Hebrews 4:15 tells us: "This High Priest of ours understands our weaknesses, for he faced all of the same testings we do, yet he did not sin."

Listen, our kids are going to be tempted. They are going to be tested. And guess what? They're going to make wrong choices and give in to their flesh—more than once—just as you have messed up and given in to your flesh more times than you can remember. But that doesn't change the fact that we are all called to be light. We can't run from the darkness; we can't hide our children away. We have to send them into the dark and equip them with the wisdom they need to dispel it with the light of Christ.

Jesus changed the world when He was on earth because He wasn't afraid to let His light shine in the midst of the darkness. Christ in your children is the hope of the world today. If you want them to shine effectively, affirm them in Christ, teach them that God is their sustainer, and continually remind them that they have been set apart and are called to live differently from the way the rest of the world lives. Then send them out to fulfill their mission as salt, light, and love.

So many young people are living in darkness. It's all they know. They're stumbling around trying to find freedom, love, and answers, and they will continue to stumble if we keep our kids, who have the capacity to bring light, under a basket.

There's no need to fear that your kids will be overcome. God's Word assures us that "the light shines in the darkness, and the darkness can never extinguish it" (John 1:5). If your children are carrying the light of Jesus within them, the darkness in the world can never extinguish it. Remember: Jochebed put Moses *in* a basket, but she didn't put him *under* one. She trusted that God had a plan for her special baby—that he would shine in the darkness and set captives free. And Pharaoh could not extinguish Moses' light.

TURN ON THE LIGHT

A few years ago eight of my friends and I decided to do a breakout room together. Do you know what that is? It's a form of game in which a group of people head into a room filled with different clues, puzzles, combination locks, and the sort. They have precisely one hour to solve all the puzzles and enter the correct combination to break out of their room. It's quite fun and addicting!

My team got the kidnapped theme room. We were blindfolded and led into a small space, and then we heard a voice telling us: "You have been kidnapped. You have an hour until your kidnapper returns. Find clues around the room left from previous victims to try and escape, or else!"

Once our countdown began, we took off our blindfolds to find that we were in a dark room handcuffed to a table. We quickly found the keys, uncuffed ourselves, and began trying to work our way through the puzzles. We solved the first two so quickly that I found myself thinking it wasn't going to be challenging enough. But it turned out to be plenty challenging.

We struggled for the next forty minutes and didn't even come close to breaking out. After the countdown expired, our host came in and walked us through all the puzzles we didn't figure out. She had been watching and listening via a video monitoring system through the whole process.

One of the first things she pointed out was the fact that we never flipped on the light switch. She said that in most groups, as soon as someone breaks out of his cuffs, he reaches over and flips on the main light so the group can see everything in the room better. #Duh! I thought the dimly lit room was part of the game, but I was wrong. Having a light to illuminate the entire room definitely would have made a difference that night.

A few days later God showed me something powerful as I was thinking about the breakout room experience. I saw people locked in different-themed rooms based on what they were struggling with—rooms such as the doubt room, the fear room, the sickness room, the hopeless room, the depression room, and the addiction room. Each room was dark, and the people inside all shared a common emotion: frustration. They were diligently trying to get out of the rooms but were having no success. Because the rooms were dark, the people were unable to get all the pieces of the puzzle in the right place. They were stuck.

What a picture of the bondage people all over our communities are experiencing! They are being held captive by the enemy, and it's our God-given responsibility as believers to get into their "rooms" and turn on the light—the light of Christ—and allow it to shine in such a way that they find their way out of bondage and into the truth that sets them free.

When we decide that we and our children are going to be who God has called us to be—the light of the world—we will help expose the enemy's tricks, schemes, and lies and help people see things more clearly. We will help them solve their puzzles, crack their codes, and break out of their frustrating existences.

LIGHT REVEALS WHAT IS LOST

Our kids must understand that eternities are at stake. They must recognize how valuable people are to God and that it is their mission to help people who are in the dark.

The parable Jesus told about the lost coin highlights God's desire for us to seek out and save the lost. My children know this parable by heart, and it fuels their purpose!

> Or suppose a woman has ten silver coins and loses one. Won't she light a lamp and sweep the entire house and search carefully until she finds it? And when she finds it, she will call in her friends and neighbors and say, "Rejoice with me because I have found my lost coin." In the same

way, there is joy in the presence of God's angels
when even one sinner repents.

—LUKE 15:8–10

This story is something all children can relate to.
If a child has ten silver quarters, and he is about to
head to the arcade, but he drops one, won't he grab his
mom's smartphone and use the flashlight feature to
search carefully until he finds it? And when he finds it,
he'll call in his brother and sister and tell them, "Yay!
I found my quarter." In the same way, heaven rejoices
when even one sinner repents.

What I love about the parable is that Jesus included
the detail about the woman's turning on the light. He
indicates that lighting a lamp would likely be the first
thing the woman would do upon losing her coin. The
light was a key element in helping her find what was
valuable to her.

In a similar way, the light that shines through our
lives is a key element in helping Jesus find what is
valuable to Him. When one of His children is far from
Him, the light can lead him back home. When one of
His children has lost his peace, the light can lead him
to the Prince of Peace. When one of His children has
lost his joy, the light can lead him back to His presence—where there is fullness of joy. When one of His
children has lost his will to live, the light can lead him
back to his purpose. When one of His children has
lost his friends, the light can lead him to the Friend
who sticks closer than a brother.

The light of our lives is Jesus shining through us.

As the moon reflects the light of the sun to a dark world, we reflect the light of Christ to a world of people in darkness. When we set our face toward Jesus and seek to know Him above all else, our lives will be like a city on a hill that can't be hidden—a city that will draw in people seeking healing, hope, and refuge. I can't imagine a better mission!

QUESTIONS FOR DISCUSSION

1. How are your children unique? Or how are you and your siblings different? Discuss the different personalities represented in your home.

2. At what age were you aware that your role in society is to be salt and light? Did your parents ever discuss your purpose with you? Have you ever struggled with an "identity crisis"?

3. How can you teach your children to shine a light in the world without their becoming like the world? Have you been fearful about the possibility of darkness extinguishing their light?

4. Share about a time when you have helped someone who was missing something valuable to him (his salvation, joy, peace, etc.) find what he was looking for by shining your light.

5. What are some practical things you can do as a family to keep your face toward Jesus so that you reflect His light and people see you as a brightly lit city on a hill?

PRAYER FOR PARENTS

Lord, I pray that You will help me to celebrate my children's unique personalities. Help me to explain to them their role in society clearly. My children are the light of the world. I will affirm who they are in Christ. I will teach them to be entirely dependent on God. I will remind them that they are set apart. I will not hide them under a basket or a bushel. I trust what Your Word says: darkness cannot extinguish the light. The light of my children's lives is Jesus, and that light cannot be extinguished. Use my children to help people who are lost find their way home. Help my children to be in the world but not of it. Give them a heart for those in the darkness who are open to the gospel, sorry for their sins, and on their way to putting their faith in Jesus. May my children reflect the light of Jesus as the moon reflects the light of the sun. May our family be like a city on a hill that cannot be hidden. In Jesus' name, amen.

CONFESSION FOR CHILDREN

I am the light of the world! The light of my life is Jesus in me. I reflect the light of Jesus as the moon reflects the light of the sun. I will let my light shine in the darkness. I will allow God to use me to find those valuable children that He is missing. I am in the world but not of it. I know I can't be an effective light if I am imitating darkness. I am a friend to sinners who are open to the gospel, sorry for their sins, and on their way to putting their faith in Jesus. People see Jesus in me. I won't keep Jesus a secret.

Chapter 9

LOVE (GOD)

A VERSE IN HABAKKUK perfectly describes the way to impart your children's purpose to them: "Write the vision; make it plain on tablets, so he may run who reads it" (2:2, ESV). Though you're not actually writing the vision, summing up your children's purpose in three words as I have in this book is exactly what Habakkuk 2:2 is talking about—making it plain. So plain that it's easy for your children to grasp and begin to fulfill their mission. When I charged my kids with their three-word purpose—salt, light, love—I saw them run with it. This simple description is so plain that even our five-year-old is running with vision!

Often we overcomplicate and over-spiritualize things, and in the process our children get confused and lose their connection with the values we are trying to instill in them. *We as parents must learn the art of turning profound spiritual truths into bite-size, kid-friendly revelation.* The more you understand the spiritual truths you're trying to impart to your children, the easier it will be to explain them to your kids. Consider this natural-realm example: I don't know how the algorithms of social media work, so I am unable to explain the algorithms of social media in plain English to my children. But I do understand how to share a picture on social media, and understanding the process makes it easy to explain it.

THE GREATEST COMMANDMENTS

In the last two chapters we sought to understand what Jesus meant when He said we are the "salt of the earth" and the "light of the world" (Matt. 5:13–14). The longer you meditate on those biblical descriptions, the more you'll understand them, and the easier it will become to make them plain to your children so they not only know that they are called to be salt, light, and love but also understand what those one-syllable words look like lived out.

We're going to spend the next two chapters seeking a revelation of the third word in our three-word purpose statement: love. Remember that significant statement I quoted previously: "The two most important days in your life are the day you are born and the day you find out why." Love is an essential piece of our "why" puzzle.

If we're going to aim our children at their God-given purpose, we must have a deep understanding of the two commandments Jesus said were the greatest: "'You must love the Lord your God with all your heart, all your soul, and all your mind.' This is the first and greatest commandment. A second is equally important: 'Love your neighbor as yourself'" (Matt. 22:37–39).

We exist to love God and to love others. This aspect of our purpose seems basic, yet many parents fail to emphasize its significance to their children, especially the first part—that we must love God with all our heart, soul, and mind. We sincerely hope our children will eventually fall in love with Jesus, but we must do more than just hope.

If you've ever seen the Disney cartoon *Aladdin*, you may remember the scene in which the genie comes out of the lamp after Aladdin rubs it and explains the terms and conditions of the three wishes he is able to grant. He informs Aladdin that he can't kill anyone, he can't make people fall in love, and he can't bring anyone back from the dead.

Just like the genie, you and I can't make anyone fall in love. We can't force our kids to love God with all their heart, soul, and mind. Entering into a loving relationship with God has to be a personal decision based on their own convictions. But we can teach them everything we know about Jesus, share our experiences of Him with them, and model the heart of our Father in such a way that when it's time for them to make that decision, it's a no-brainer. As parents we are privileged to have the ability to shape our children's convictions.

Although the genie couldn't make Jasmine fall in love with Aladdin, he did help her take notice of him. What are you doing to help your children take notice of God? What are you doing to strengthen your children's personal relationship with the Trinity? Are your kids even aware that they can have a personal relationship with Jesus, or are they living vicariously through you?

There's a whole new world out there—and it's not for storybook characters. God has an incredible adventure for your children—plans that are far beyond all you could ask, think, or imagine for them—and those plans kick into gear when they decide to live for God and love Him with every fiber of their beings. It's up to you to present an irresistible Jesus to your kids so they will surrender their lives to Him without question.

The more real, approachable, and loving we make the throne of God, the more time our children will spend there. And the more time they spend there, the more they will fall in love with Jesus. And the more they fall in love with Jesus, the more secure in their purpose—to love God with all their heart, soul, and mind—they'll become.

TEACH THEM WHILE THEY ARE YOUNG

The older our children get, the more difficult it becomes to keep Jesus the center of their focus, because video games, friends, sports, smartphones, and a million other things are vying for their attention. As adults we struggle with these distractions as well.

Studies show Americans log into their iPhones eighty times per day, accessing them on average every twelve minutes.[1] We touch, swipe, scroll, pinch, and pull the addictive things 2,617 times a day on average.[2] From push notifications to calendar invites to never-ending email threads, the digital environment is continually begging for more of our time. Did you know that the average attention span is believed to have fallen to eight seconds, down from twelve in the year 2000?[3] Apparently we now have a shorter attention span than a goldfish! Satya Nadella, the chief executive officer of Microsoft, was recently quoted as saying "the true scarce commodity" of the near future will be "human attention."[4] In other words, the thing that will be the hardest to come by in the not-too-distant future will be our ability to focus without being distracted.

We must push against the current of the distracted culture in which we live. Jesus came to set the captives free, but many of us are held captive by digital devices that we have the ability to walk away from. We must guard our hearts and teach our children to guard theirs. You can't guard their hearts for them. And as God's Word points out, guarding one's heart is of paramount importance: "Above all else, guard your heart, for everything you do flows from it" (Prov. 4:23, NIV). This truth bears repeating: *Everything we do flows from our hearts.*

When our children mess up, it's easy to look at their external behavior and put all our efforts into eradicating that behavior, but we should be more concerned about what's going on internally than what we are seeing externally. If you're dealing with sinful or rebellious children, it's because somewhere along the line they took God off the throne of their hearts and replaced Him with someone or something else. It's usually a slow process and undetected by many, but what has happened is that over time they have let their guard down and gone from worshipping God to worshipping an idol.

God is passionate, and He created us to be passionate people, but unfortunately we are prone to misdirect our passion. We exist to love God with all our heart, soul, and mind, and when we aren't doing that, we're bound to have issues. In the same way my car, which is designed to run on gasoline, would have issues if I started filling the fuel tank with soda pop.

MISPLACED AFFECTION

Paul wrote to the church at Corinth about the dangers of misplacing our passion. "Therefore, my beloved, run [keep far, far away] from [any sort of] idolatry [and that includes loving anything more than God, or participating in anything that leads to sin and enslaves the soul]" (1 Cor. 10:14, AMP).

I know you love your children. You love them deeply, or you never would have picked up this book. They are your beloved, and you must warn them as Paul warned the church at Corinth, which he loved. We must warn our children to run from idolatry. When I hear the word *idol*, my imagination conjures up images of gold statues that would look great on the set of *Indiana Jones*, but that's not the type of idol Paul is referring to. An idol is anything that we love more than God.

John Calvin once wrote that the human mind is "a perpetual forge of idols." Almost since the world began, mankind has been "forging gods at will," he said. "The human mind, stuffed as it is with presumptuous rashness, dares to imagine a god suited to its own capacity; as it labours under dullness, nay, is sunk in the grossest ignorance, it substitutes vanity and an empty phantom in the place of God."[5] His statement makes it clear that innumerable idols are vying for God's place in our minds and hearts.

I think it's safe to say that no one in the history of humanity has ever made an idol out of broccoli. Why? Because broccoli isn't all that great. I can say without hesitation that broccoli has never vied for the seat of my heart. (Now, chocolate—that's a different matter!)

Seriously, what "loves" put us in the danger zone? I have heard it said that the greatest danger to best comes from second best. God is best in my life, but what is second best? Whatever is second best is the very thing that will creep in and take God's rightful place as the King of my heart. For me, second best is my relationship with my husband and my kids. I have to be mindful that I don't let my love for them over-shadow my love for God.

Jesus knew this would be an issue for us, so He addressed it: "The person who loves his father or mother more than me does not deserve to be my disciple. The person who loves a son or daughter more than me does not deserve to be my disciple" (Matt. 10:37, GW).

Those are serious declarations, but Jesus knew that the greatest danger to best is second best, so He had to warn us. We can't prefer our spouse, our family, our friends, our career, our smartphones, or anything else over Him. We are to love Him with all our heart, soul, and mind.

We need to identify the second-best things in our children's lives and talk to them about the genuine risk of those second-best things taking the place of God in their lives. It could be their sports team, their friends, their video game system, their boyfriend or girlfriend, their car, or their report card—all good things, but things that will cause them to stumble if they begin to cling to and rely on those things. Nothing will derail the plans and purposes that God has for us like removing Him from the center of our heart's affection.

Whatever our hearts cling to and rely upon, *that* is our God.

I can cling to and rely on my family for love, support, affirmation, and joy, but my family is not perfect and therefore can't meet my needs for love, support, affirmation, and joy. I can't make them little gods. As wonderful as they are, they will only disappoint me if I put them on the throne of my heart. God doesn't warn us to run from idols because He's worried about being ditched; He warns us because He knows people and things will never satisfy us. That's the way He designed us.

There is only one worthy to be clung to and relied upon, and His name is Jesus.

Highlight that statement. It is one of the single most significant truths you can ever impart to your children. Friends will let them down. Coaches will let them down. You will let them down. Their education will let them down. Everyone and everything will let them down at some point—except God. He will never fail them. If we could learn to depend on God for everything, we would never be disappointed again.

Keep pointing your kids back to Jesus. Keep asking questions about where their affections lie. They need your perspective. They need you to help them stay focused. They need you to aim them in the right direction.

WORSHIP KEEPS US FOCUSED

One of the best ways to keep your children's passion for the Lord from fizzling is to teach them how to worship God. Worship is love expressed, and if our families are continually expressing love to God, we won't have to worry about other things coming along and taking His place. Worship is a beautiful way to remind God, yourself, and the enemy that your heart belongs fully to God.

Many churchgoers put worship in a box. Worship becomes nothing more than singing the latest Hillsong or Elevation Worship song on a Sunday morning with our church family. We clap, we raise our hands, we close our eyes, we hit our knees, we maybe even tear up a little. But then the song ends, and we hear a message, go home, and wait seven days to "worship" again.

Worship is so much more than singing songs at church! That's a part of it, certainly—one of my favorite parts. I love corporate worship. But worship should be happening all day, every day, wherever we are—in our secret places, around the dinner table, in our cars, and under our breath. We have to go full on "Skidamarink." Remember that preschool song? It talks about loving someone all day long.

Let's love God all day long. Let's be a people who worship Him around the clock. Have you told God lately that you love Him? Have you told Him that there is no one else above Him?

Paul puts it a bit differently: "So here's what I want you to do, God helping you: Take your everyday, ordinary life—your sleeping, eating, going-to-work, and walking-around life—and place it before God as an offering. Embracing what God does for you is the best thing you can do for him" (Rom. 12:1, MSG).

Are we embracing what God does for us? We must enthusiastically accept each new day we've been given as the extravagant gift that it is and hold closely the promises given to us. Our lives should embrace all that God has done, will do, and is doing in our lives! All things are from Him, to Him, and through Him; therefore, all our praise belongs to Him.

Take time as a family to worship God together at church and outside church. Sing songs together in the car on the way to school or work, or forget the music and thank God out loud together. Keep Jesus at the center by keeping praise and worship at the forefront.

Invest in some children's worship music. Our favorite resource is Ken Blount Ministries. I love the simple and powerful truths found in Ken's music. My husband helped write and produce many of the songs, and I've seen firsthand how quickly the lyrics take root in little, fertile hearts.

We also have several worship playlists on Spotify featuring our family's favorite worship songs—from those sung by artists such as Lauren Daigle, Kari Jobe, and Rita Springer to those sung by groups such as Upperroom, Elevation, and Hillsong.

Last year I listened to 40,958 minutes of music. Many of those minutes were spent listening to worship music. I spent sixty-eight hours listening to Elevation Worship alone. Was I engaged and worshipping during every one of those sixty-eight hours? No. But even when the songs were just background music, my kids were picking up on the lyrics, and you never know when those lyrics might spring up in their minds and hearts at just the right time, reminding them of God's Word and His faithfulness. We need to teach our children that we don't worship to get things from God, but because He is so very good, He always shows up and ministers to us in exactly the way we need Him to.

GAINING ACCESS TO GOD

The Bible tells us how we are to approach God. "Enter his gates with thanksgiving, and his courts with praise! Give thanks to him; bless his name!" (Ps. 100:4, ESV). I love the way *The Message* words this verse: "Enter with the password: 'Thank you!' *Make yours*elves at home, talking praise. Thank him. Worship him."

I can definitely identify with the concept of using a password. Everything is password protected these days! If I want to get into my iPhone, open my garage,

145

or log into my Amazon account, I have to enter my password. God's presence has always been password protected, but the password isn't a secret. He tells us precisely what we need to say to enter into His fantastic presence. The password is "Thank You!"

Thanksgiving and praise

We must teach our kids that thanksgiving gets us into God's dwelling place and praise gets us all the way up to His throne. We gain special access to Him when we have an attitude of thanksgiving. When we live a life of gratitude, a life that is always offering up praise, we get a VIP pass that puts us ahead of the common believer and allows us to walk right into His courts.

I can tell you from firsthand experience that the time you spend with God in His courts will take your relationship with Him to a new level. Thanksgiving opens doors to greater dimensions of God. It moves your seat from the nosebleed section to courtside, and Psalm 84 says *one* day in His courts is better than a *thousand* anywhere else!

I don't know about you, but I want my family to live in God's courts. I want to dwell in His presence and at His feet surrounded by my husband and children because the more we worship Him, the more we know Him; and the more we know Him, the more secure His place in our hearts becomes.

Obedience

Another way we can help our children make sure that God stays on the throne of their hearts is teaching them the importance of obedience. Jesus told His disciples, "If you love me, you will obey my commandments" (John 14:15, GW).

Loving God is more than a feeling. It's more than words. It's more than worship. It's joyful obedience. Jesus said so Himself: "If you love Me, you will obey My commandments." When our children are rebelling and sinning, it's because they have fallen out of love or perhaps were never in love with Him in the first place. Our children must possess a pure motive for obedience, and it's our responsibility to shape their motive. In doing so, we must train them to obey not out of fear or the expectation of a reward but out of *love*. We want them to have a heart that says, "I will obey because I want to show God how much I love Him, not because I am afraid of punishment or looking for affirmation."

Obedience is love expressed. This truth will move you from surface-level parenting to kingdom-minded parenting. We're not of this world, so we cannot parent our children as the rest of the world does. The world demands, "Obey or get punished." God counters, "Obey because you love Me." We can't top God's motive. It's so pure. It's so right. It's so God-centered. It's so elementary. It helps us to view obedience as an incredible privilege and the way we show God how much He means to us—rather than as a burden.

Jesus had more to say to children about obedience

than that they are to demonstrate their love for Him by obeying Him. He also told them to obey their parents. "Children, obey your parents because you belong to the Lord, for this is the right thing to do" (Eph. 6:1).

Jesus said we are to love Him with all our heart, soul, and mind and that if we love Him, we will obey His commandments. He has commanded your children to obey you—not because you are perfect, not because they don't want to get grounded, not because they want a sticker or an allowance, but because they love Him. This is something we need to verbalize continually in our homes: if you love God, you will obey your parents.

Map this out for your children. Take them through the Bible. Show them Matthew 22:37. Show them the great and supreme command—a gigantic piece of their purpose puzzle. Then take them to John 14:15. Show them where in the Scriptures Jesus said obedience equals loving Him. Then take them to Ephesians 6:1. Show them that Jesus commanded children to obey their parents.

If your children can grasp that obedience is a way of expressing love toward God, it will change the atmosphere of your home forever. And can you imagine the energy that you will save not having to come up with ways to motivate your children to obey? This is a game changer, friends.

The bull's-eye you're aiming your kids at will determine what they believe their purpose to be. Aim them toward loving God with all their heart, soul, and mind.

QUESTIONS FOR DISCUSSION

1. We learned that the greatest threat to what is best comes from what is second best. What is your second best? What competes for the throne of your heart?

2. If we want to aim our children toward loving God, we must warn them about idolatry. What or who do you think is your child's second best right now? What or who is fighting for his heart?

3. Worship is love expressed. Describe what your worship life looks like. What are some ways you can take your family with you into the courts of God?

4. If we love God, we will obey Him. What have you been using to motivate your children to obey?

5. Have you ever thought of obedience as worship? Describe how you think motivating your children to obey because they love God might change the atmosphere of your home.

PRAYER FOR PARENTS

Lord, help me aim my children toward loving You with all their heart, soul, and mind. I know I can't force them to love You, but I also know I can help them notice You, experience You, and can draw them to You by modeling Your love. Help us to guard our hearts. You and You alone belong on the throne of my heart. I choose to rely on You and You alone. I will cling to You and You alone. I will run from idolatry. Help me to recognize the things in my children that are second best—the things that are vying for the throne of their hearts. We will be a family that worships You more than once a week. May our home be filled with thanksgiving and praise. Help us to lead the way in this. I want to spend every day in Your courts. I want more of You, and I know where to find it—at Your feet, in Your courts. I will worship You with obedience. I will motivate my children to obey because they love You. Thank You, Lord, for thinking of everything. You hold the answers to all my questions. I love You. In Jesus' name, amen.

CONFESSION FOR CHILDREN

I love the Lord my God with all my heart, with all my soul, and with all my mind. I will run from idolatry—anything that takes God's place in my life. I rely on God for everything. I cling to God and God alone. People will disappoint me, but God never will, so I purpose to keep Him on the throne of my heart. I express my love to God through worship and obedience. I worship Him because He is worthy of my praise. I love Him all day long. I will show Him that I love Him by obeying His commands. I don't obey God for reward or for fear of punishment; I obey God because it's how I show Him that I love Him. He has commanded me to obey my parents, and because I love God, I will obey them.

Chapter 10

LOVE (OTHERS)

A S WE SAW in the last chapter, Jesus told us that the first and greatest command is to love God with all our heart, soul, and mind. He said the second is *equally* important—to love our neighbors as ourselves. (See Matthew 22:37–39.)

The only chance our kids have at being the salt of the earth and the light of the world is to love God *and* others. In other words, they cannot fulfill their purpose without love. Sometimes we confuse being salt and light with being snarky and judgmental. I went to public school, and I remember the Christian kids who looked down on everyone. It was obvious they thought they were better and holier than everyone else, and as a result, they never made an impact on anyone. The Bible says it is God's kindness that leads men to repentance (see Romans 2:4, ESV)—not a person's judgmental or superior attitude. When these kids who lacked love tried to be salt and light, their efforts bore no fruit. They were simply, as the apostle Paul described those without love, "a noisy gong or a clanging cymbal" (1 Cor. 13:1).

I am not sure what kind of power my mom has

that's enabled her to do this—but I'm convinced it is something superhuman. Every toy, baby doll, board game, VHS tape, or book that my siblings and I owned growing up is still at her house and in close to mint condition. I assure you, it's not because we did not play with the toys—we did! All seven of us kids and all twenty-plus grandchildren have played with them, yet they're still in excellent condition, and my children's children will probably play with them someday.

One of the toys that has been around forever is the 1979 Fisher-Price Marching Band set. It's a red drum that holds a set of lime-green maracas, a yellow tambourine, yellow drumsticks, and shiny, red-handled cymbals. It's been in the family since before I was born. It's a great toy—until the baby playing with it discovers how to use the red-handled cymbals. Then it becomes the *worst* toy ever.

I don't care how cute the baby is, when they start clanging together those two cymbals, the noise is awful. You want to leave the room and close the door tightly behind you. You know that to keep your sanity, you must get away.

Before Paul paints a beautiful picture of what love is, he warns the church at Corinth: "If you don't love others—your words will be like a clanging cymbal." (See 1 Corinthians 13:1.) He's essentially saying, "People will avoid you—they'll close the door on you. You will lose your influence." That's a sobering thought. If we're not influencing anyone, we're not fulfilling our God-given destiny. We must filter every word we speak and every action we take through love.

Salt. Light. Love.

Salt without love doesn't enhance God-flavors; instead it makes them unpalatable. Light without love doesn't help people find their way; instead it blinds them with its harshness.

What Is Love?

How does God define "love"? Let's take a closer look at what His Word says and ask Him to search our hearts for anything that displeases Him.

> Love is patient and kind. Love is not jealous or boastful or proud or rude. It does not demand its own way. It is not irritable, and it keeps no record of being wronged. It does not rejoice about injustice but rejoices whenever the truth wins out. Love never gives up, never loses faith, is always hopeful, and endures through every circumstance.
>
> —1 Corinthians 13:4–7

We live in a world that seems more concerned about how love *feels* than about what loves *does;* but notice, Paul doesn't mention anything about how love feels in these verses. Instead he describes what love looks like in action. True love is more than words or emotions. True love is demonstrated by action. Do you see these actions in your kids? If not, they probably aren't seeing these actions in you.

Love is patient.

Patience is likened to a candle with a very long wick that allows it to burn for a long time. How is your patience? Would those who know you best use that image to describe you? Would your kids say that you're patient with them? Would your spouse say you're patient with him or her? Does anyone ever tell you, "Thanks for being patient with me"? Colossians 3:12 says we must clothe ourselves in patience. It doesn't come standard. We must *choose* to put it on. One of the ways I can tell I have neglected to put on patience is by how snappy my responses to people are.

When I was seventeen, a few months before getting married, I decided while working at a clothing store that the retail world was not for me, so I started looking in the paper for a new job. The paper—that makes me sound so old! But it's the truth. I saw a listing for a receptionist at a tax firm, and I have no idea why, but I applied for the job and got it. I worked there for several years. It was a small tax firm—five employees total—and one of the people I worked with was an older gentleman I'll call Sam.

In addition to having ninja-like calculator skills, Sam was also a runner. He ran faithfully every day, and he also stretched faithfully every day. I know because my desk was near the fax machine, and every time Sam came back to fax something, he would go through a series of stretches while he waited for his fax to go through. Stretching was an important part of Sam's routine because he understood that if he was not regularly stretching, something was going to snap.

Warm and limber muscles keep pulled hamstrings and torn ligaments at bay.

Hebrews 12:2 says that as believers, we are running a race. And since we are running a race, we have to remember to stretch—daily—because if we are not taking time to stretch, we are going to find ourselves snapping at the people we love most and the people God placed in our paths to minister to.

The tighter your muscles are, the greater chance you have for injury. Sam never had a running injury the entire time I worked at that tax firm, and I believe it was because he took advantage of every opportunity to stretch. Stretching lengthens and elongates our muscles. We are called to have long wicks, to be long-suffering, to be patient and not irritable. We are called to be the opposite of snappy. So how do we stretch?

First we stretch down. We get down on our knees or at least assume an inward posture that shows God we are submitted to Him and His Word. We remind ourselves that His Word has the final word in our lives and that without Him, we would go astray.

Then we stretch up. We extend our hands and our hearts toward heaven and begin to worship God for who He is. We express our love to Him. We enter into His presence by being thankful for the cross, His love, and His hand on our lives.

Lastly we stretch out. We reach out as the hands and feet of Jesus. We ask God to use us, and when He gives us an opportunity to partner with Him to bring heaven to earth, we take it.

I promise that if you will take time to stretch down,

up, and out every day, several times a day, you will see your patience increase and your irritability decrease. When you are faxing something, driving to a meeting, on the way home from work, or in the shower—stretch down, stretch up, stretch out. Elongate your patience muscles, and you'll be less likely to snap when life or people are trying.

When you notice your kids are snappy, talk to them about the importance of stretching and teach them how to do it. On the way to school, stretch together. After a tough football game, stretch together. When your children are fighting with one another, stretch together. Stretch together when things feel tight; stretch together when things are going great. The more we stretch, the less likely we are to lose our patience and injure those we are supposed to influence.

Love is kind. Love does not demand its own way and is not rude.

When I think of kindness, I think of Big Bird from the preschool TV program *Sesame Street*, kindergarten teachers, and people who ring bells during Christmas as they collect donations for the Salvation Army. But being kind is more than baking cookies for your new neighbors. The word translated "kindness" in Galatians 5:22–23, which lists the fruit of the Spirit, likens it to wine that has grown mellow with age and lost its harshness.[1] Kind people are people who have lost their harshness, don't demand their own way, and are not rude. Kindness also describes people who adapt well to others.

According to the Merriam-Webster English Language Learner's Dictionary, *adapt* means "to change your behavior so that it is easier to live in a particular place or situation."[2] If love is kind, then it adapts.

What are you changing about your behavior to make it easier for those you live with, work with, and do life with to live with, work with, and do life—with *you*? People in general are resistant to change. We get comfortable, and we like things to be as they've always been—including our personalities. Being comfortable in our own skin seems like a life goal, but if our own skin includes attitudes that cause us to forfeit our ability to reach others, it's time to get uncomfortable.

We like to defend character flaws with excuses such as, "This is just the way God made me." "I'm opinionated—it's just the way God made me." "I'm not very empathetic—it's just the way God made me." "I'm controlling—it's just the way God made me." "I'm an introvert—it's just the way God made me." "I'm an extrovert—it's just the way God made me." "I'm dramatic—it's just the way God made me."

We want everyone around us to adapt to the way God created us, but kindness is the willingness to lay down our natural tendencies to adapt to those around us and love them as Jesus would love them. We say we want to be the hands and feet of Jesus—but is that only if we get to do it on our terms? *When our God-given strengths start becoming excuses for why we can't do what God is asking us to do, they are no longer strengths but weaknesses.*

Because it can be difficult for us to notice when we've settled into a "this is just the way I am" mentality, it's vital that we regularly ask people we trust if they have noticed our being harsh, demanding, rude, or unwilling to adapt.

Our family is made up of five highly opinionated people. If you don't like the same movies, restaurants, and music we like—you're wrong. Of course that way of thinking is going to rub certain people the wrong way. And while we might try to comfort ourselves by saying that Jesus rubbed people the wrong way, we must remember that although Jesus did ruffle feathers, He did so only when it came to eternal issues.

Jesus adapted to reach those around Him. He left behind heaven and adapted as no one has ever adapted before or since. He changed His DNA. He changed His makeup. He changed His address. He became like us so that He could rescue us. Let's quit being so stubborn and set in our ways—let's be adaptable instead. Let's be kind, and let's help God rescue those who still need rescuing.

When you notice your children laying down their preferred way of doing things to serve another, celebrate that! As parents we usually spend more time pointing out bad behavior than recognizing when love is at work—but the more we acknowledge kindness in our children and celebrate it, the more value they will place on it. When you see your older child, who wants to play Clue, adapt to your younger child, who wants to play Candy Land, don't forget to pull your older child aside and commend him for demonstrating kindness. Let him know he lived out a 1 Corinthians 13 kind of love.

Love is not jealous.

Jealousy causes us to rejoice about injustice, but love rejoices whenever the truth wins out. Jealousy is dangerous. Jealousy murdered Abel. Jealousy threw Joseph in a pit and then sold him into slavery. Jealousy nailed Jesus to the cross.

> So when they had assembled [for this purpose], Pilate said to them, "Whom do you want me to set free for you? Barabbas, or Jesus who is called Christ?" For Pilate knew that *it was because of jealousy* that the chief priests and elders had handed Jesus over to him.
> —MATTHEW 27:17–18, AMP, EMPHASIS ADDED

Jealousy makes people do crazy things! Jealousy and love cannot coexist. I've seen jealousy ruin friendships. I know two friends who used to get along swimmingly until one of those friends began to gain more influence. The other friend wanted that kind of influence. She pretended to be happy for her friend, but jealousy was eating her alive. She became like Saul, and although she didn't try to murder her friend as Saul tried to murder David, she did things to try to kill her friend's influence. Her own family, her own platform, her calling—it wasn't enough. She wanted what her friend had, and her jealousy ultimately destroyed their friendship.

When I was growing up, people led much more

private lives. I mean, sure, you knew when your friend's parents got a new car, but I didn't know where my friends were vacationing and how often. My parents didn't know about every date night their friends were going on or every award their friend's children received at school. We didn't know when people were hanging out without us or that we hadn't been invited to this or that. And we were happy not knowing. But today, access to a continual feed of the world's highlight reels is right at our fingertips—and those highlight reels are a perfect breeding ground for jealousy.

Think about it. You see a picture of a girl you went to high school with on a social media site and she's had three kids, same as you, but she still looks flawless in her two-piece. You heart her photo, wishing you looked like her. You see a picture of a beautiful Christmas tree in a tidy house, and you heart the photo, wishing you had a tidy house and a tree that stunning. You see a picture of your friends from church on vacation, smiling and making lifelong memories— and you heart the photo, all the while wishing you had enough money to go on vacation and that you had a family you felt like making lifelong memories with. Your thoughts seem harmless, but as you scroll and heart and wish for an Instagram-worthy life, jealousy is contaminating your soul and affecting your ability to love. If we want to actually love people and not just heart their pictures, we have to deal with our jealousy. We have to get to the root, and the root of jealousy is unthankfulness.

I wonder how differently the story about the two

friends would have ended if instead of letting jealousy dictate her actions, the one friend recognized that she was dealing with envy and was honest, repentant, and thankful. What if she had been thankful not only for how God was using her friend but also grateful for God's faithfulness in her own life—thankful in her confidence that her season would come and that until then she could stand beside her friend and be a pillar of support?

Thankfulness changes everything.

We must train our children to be thankful—in all circumstances! Grateful people rarely struggle with jealousy because they spend more time thanking God for what they have than wasting time wishing for what others have. If I'm jealous of what God is doing in your life, I will struggle to love you with Christlike love. But if I'm thankful for what God is doing in your life, I can love you with a love that sticks closer than a brother.

I know it's difficult for a teenage girl to be thankful when her friend got invited to a slumber party and she didn't—but if she will push jealousy aside and choose to find something to be grateful for instead of letting envy create division in their friendship, she will learn how powerful 1 Corinthians 13 love really is.

Love is not boastful or prideful.

Disneyland in Anaheim, California, is my favorite place on earth. My husband, Josh, and I have been vacationing there since we were first married, and every time we visit, I fall in love with it a little bit more.

There's just something special about leaving the real world behind for four or five days and entering into a land where you can't help but feel like a kid again.

If there happens to be a parade on a day that we're visiting, you'll find me sitting on a curb a good hour before the parade starts to ensure a great seat—eating a churro and smiling as I wait for iconic Disney and Pixar characters such as Mickey, Minnie, Cinderella, Sulley, and Mr. Incredible to ride up on impressive floats. When the parade kicks off, it's the center of attention. Even if you don't get a front-row curb seat, you can still see what's going on. The floats are elaborate, and some reach up to thirty feet in the air, so all who come to this happy place can see and enjoy Princess Elsa waving and blowing kisses to Olaf. The parade is not a private event. If you're walking by, even if you aren't intentionally attending the parade, you can see and hear what's going on.

What's my point? A parade is appropriate in an amusement park, but it's not characteristic of true love. First Corinthians 13:4 says "love does not parade itself" (NKJV). Love doesn't brag or seek attention. It doesn't need an audience. Love is not about the limelight, and it does not show off.

Thanks to social media, we live in a day in which parading is easier than ever and widely accepted. I'm not saying there is anything wrong with sharing acts of love on social media—*if* our motives are pure. We have to check them constantly. Did we "love" that person or that organization so we could parade our good heart on Instagram and enjoy being the center of attention for fifteen minutes? Would we have done what we did if no one were watching? Can we be satisfied loving someone with a Christlike love even if we must remain anonymous? Or do we need the hearts, likes, and affirmation of others to experience gratification? Yes, we must share our acts of love—but with a right heart. Are we parading or hoping to inspire? Love is OK with not being recognized.

We must teach our children to check their motives continually as well. Am I doing what I'm doing to gain popularity or approval or to beef up my college application? Am I doing it because I want to be like Jesus? Am I doing it to make up for the bad thing I did earlier this week? Or am I doing it because God has been good to me and I want to share His love with others? If we ask our kids the right questions, the Holy Spirit will illuminate wrong motives and lead them to repentance. He will empower them to love others without pride's clouding everything up!

Love keeps no record of wrongs.

I honestly don't get the point of playing a game in which there are no winners or losers and the score doesn't matter. I don't buy the line, "It's just for fun!" If I play a game, I play to win, and if I know up front that at the end of the game a winner won't be identified, then I don't want to play the game. Christmas trivia, tic-tac-toe, charades—you name it—in my view, every game needs a scoreboard.

Love, however, is not a game, and to be all in, we must throw out the internal scoreboards that keep track of how many times someone has wronged us. This is very difficult to do, especially for a competitive person like me. The Holy Spirit has had to show me several times that I was unconsciously keeping records of wrongs.

I did this for several years in my relationship with my husband. I have known for as long as Josh and I have been married that the number one way he receives love is through words of affirmation. I genuinely believe that's why he fell in love with me in the first place. I used to dote on him with my words to such an extent that I'm sure he was convinced he was the greatest human I had ever met.

We've now been married almost sixteen years, and over the last ten to twelve, the words of affirmation have not always rolled off my tongue as they should, especially since I know how important they are to him. I know because we have had many conversations in which I asked him what I can do to better serve him as a wife, and he asked me what he can do to better serve me as a husband. His answer always included something about needing more encouragement from me. I would try to do better, but it still felt forced and fake. Not because he isn't unbelievably amazing. I truly believe in my heart of hearts that he is the best husband anywhere, ever! But the words of affirmation didn't flow from me as they once had.

God began to deal with me about this. I was deeply convicted and finally realized this was an area I couldn't improve in my own strength or by reading another book about how important honor and words are to your husband. I sat on my couch early one morning and told the Lord I wasn't leaving until He showed me why I withheld words of encouragement from the one person I love most on the earth.

The Spirit of God rushed in. I've heard people talk about being "undone" before the Lord, and I always wondered what they meant by that—until that morning. I was truly undone. It was as if God came in and took a tangled-up knot in my heart, untangled it all in an instant, and revealed to me the secrets of my heart.

All at once I knew with an undeniable knowing that the reason I had been stingy with my words was that I was subconsciously trying to hurt Josh. I was trying to make him pay for the time early in our marriage when a pornography addiction had reared its ugly head and deeply wounded me. I thought I had completely forgiven him, but without realizing it, I had made the decision to hurt him by withholding my affirmation. In my heart the score wasn't even yet, and I was trying to balance it by dishing out wrong for wrong. I was keeping a record of the ways and times in which Josh had wounded me. I never sat down and thought through this evil plan to hurt him and make him feel a little of what I felt. No, this was a secret plan, a plan *I* didn't even know about!

My experience shows how important it is for us to ask the Holy Spirit to reveal whether we have a secret scoreboard in our hearts—and if we do, to ask Him to dismantle it! When we have moments of undoing like the one I had on my couch, we will naturally want to lead our kids to the same place of freedom. We have no idea what hurtful things our children are holding on to. We have no clue what records of wrong they are keeping. They may not even realize themselves that they have a hidden scoreboard; the Bible says we can't know our own hearts. (See Jeremiah 17:9, NKJV.)

But Spirit-led parents can help their children discover their secret scoreboards. Here's how: At bedtime every once in a while, tell your children to ask the Holy Spirit whether they have any unforgiveness in their hearts that they need to give over to God. They may be angry with you for something you said months ago. They may be holding on to some hurtful words that someone spoke to or about them at school. They may be frustrated with themselves for a mistake they made. The Holy Spirit knows, and He will show them because He is just as much *their* helper as He is *your* helper.

Think about how much heartache and bitterness might have been spared if only you knew to check with the Holy Spirit as a child and ask Him to show you if you were keeping any records of wrongs! He will not only show us the records we are keeping but also help us wipe them clean and step into new levels of freedom. If we want our children to walk in love, we must teach them what true forgiveness looks like.

Love never gives up, never loses faith, is always hopeful, and endures through every circumstance.

People make it easy for us to give up on them. They let us down over and over again. They frustrate us. They don't get it when we want them to get it! Sometimes when we see them "going around the mountain" one more time, we can't help but think, *Like, for real, why don't you get a clue? It's so obvious. You know God's Word. You know what to do. You've been going to the same church I have for the last five years—how are you still not getting it? Are we really having this same conversation again?*

We want to wash our hands of people who aren't getting it and be done with them. We pray, "God, I've done all I know to do, I've said all I know to say, so here You go." But that's not love. Love never gives up. Love never considers someone too far gone. Love never loses faith in people. Love is hopeful that God can bring transformation! Love endures through every circumstance.

Aren't you thankful that God has never given up on you? That He has never lost faith in you and that He is filled with hope about your future in Him? Aren't you thankful that His love endures through every circumstance? When we remind ourselves of how God loves us, it fills our hearts with grace and allows us to love those people our flesh wants to cut off.

Your kids need to hear hope in your voice when you talk about your sister who is lost. Your kids need to hear you fight in prayer for the people who frustrate you most. Invite them into the process.

One of my friends has been praying for her husband's side of the family for several years. She knew God had more for them. She brought her young daughters into the process. They prayed together on a regular basis for these family members who would have been easy to give up on, and because God leans down and listens when we pray, and because His Word doesn't return void, they have experienced a *true* miracle in their family—and my friend's young daughters got to be a part of it!

I believe as you teach your kids that love never gives up, as you pray with them and talk with them, their pure hearts will minister to you. Your children can help you see people with a fresh, godly perspective. What a gift to be able to see people we have all but given up on with a different set of hope-filled eyes! The Bible tells us that even our best vision is nothing more than a reflection of reality.

> For now we see but a faint reflection of riddles and mysteries as though reflected in a mirror, but one day we will see face-to-face. My understanding is incomplete now, but one day I will understand everything, just as everything about me has been fully understood. Until then, there are three things that remain: faith, hope, and love—yet love surpasses them all. So above all else, let love be the beautiful prize for which you run.
> —1 CORINTHIANS 13:12–13, TPT

Let love be the beautiful prize that our children run for—and let's run right there beside them!

QUESTIONS FOR DISCUSSION

1. Does your family have a vision statement? Discuss why having a three-word vision statement will make it easier for your children to fulfill God's call on their lives.

2. Love is patient, and love is not irritable. How would you describe your patience level? Discuss how you will incorporate stretching through your day and with your children.

3. Does your family have a difficult time adapting to love others? Have you ever excused your tendency to offend people with your personality by saying, "It's just the way God made me"?

4. Jealousy is dangerous. What are your jealousy triggers? Do your kids have jealousy triggers? In other words, who or what seems to stir up the dangerous emotion of jealousy in your hearts? What are you most thankful for in this season of life?

5. Are you an internal scorekeeper? Share how you plan to teach your children to ask the Holy Spirit to reveal the secrets of their hearts.

Prayer for Parents

Lord, help me to model 1 Corinthians 13 love for my children. I want love to be the beautiful prize for which I run. Help me to be patient. Holy Spirit, I give You permission to speak to me and show me when I am being snappy and need to stretch down, up, and out. I ask You for a spirit of kindness to be present in our home. Show me how to adapt to others. Rid me of harshness. Holy Spirit, help me not to be demanding. I want nothing to do with jealousy, so I will choose to be thankful for what I have. I will be content and quit wishing for what others have. As I seek You, keep my motives pure. Make me aware when I am parading and boasting. I am fulfilled by You, not by the praise and affirmation of others. I choose this day to throw out all my internal scoreboards.

I desire not to keep records of wrongs, and I trust You with every corner of my heart. Help me to be a person who doesn't give up on others, doesn't lose faith in people, is hopeful, and endures through every circumstance. I refuse to be a clanging cymbal—I will love others as Christ has loved me. In Jesus' name, amen.

CONFESSION FOR CHILDREN

Love is my goal. I know I can't lead anyone to Jesus without His love working through me. God's love never gives up, and it cares more for others than for self. Love is not jealous. Love does not parade itself. Love is not "me first." Love is slow to anger and doesn't keep score when people mess up. Love doesn't rejoice when others are hurting. Love trusts God always. Love doesn't look back and believes the best. Today I will be salt, light, and love.

Chapter 11

DOERS OF
THE WORD

EVERYONE REMEMBERS HOW exciting it is to turn sixteen. I mean, even if you don't get a car right away, just knowing you're old enough to drive is exhilarating. I'll be honest: I didn't retain much of anything from my driver's education course. I know I passed the written exam, but I probably remembered only about 20 percent of what my passionless instructor presented. I didn't learn to drive sitting in a depressing, windowless classroom listening to someone talk about the ins and outs of driving. I learned to drive sitting behind the wheel of an actual car!

I'm sure the same was true for you. You learned how to signal, brake, turn on the windshield wipers, change lanes, and parallel park because you got in a car with a brave parent or instructor who taught you how to do all those things. And then you did them again and again until finally you were confident enough to take your behind-the-wheel test and become a licensed driver.

The Department of Motor Vehicles is not going to hand anyone a license simply because he can quote the driver's ed manual word for word. No, they have to see that a person applying for a license can actually *put into practice* what the manual says about how to drive. Head knowledge alone is not enough.

It's the same for medical professionals as it is for drivers. Aren't you glad doctors participate in clinicals when they are in medical school? Clinicals provide practice experiences "that allow students to understand, perform, and refine professional competencies at the appropriate program level."[1] It's hands-on, real-life experience. It's important that medical students hit the books, memorize loads of information, and take written tests, but the real understanding comes through clinicals. The practical experience allows them to apply the book knowledge to real life-or-death situations.

A friend of mine who is a pediatric intensive care nurse shared with me that there is no way she could have learned to interact with patients and their families from reading a textbook. Problem-solving and prioritizing aren't learned in the classroom. Hearing a nurse educator talk about how to handle a child who is panicking when you are trying to put in an IV is not nearly as helpful as watching a person handle such a child. To acquire practical skills, you must actually apply the head knowledge you've gained. I know I'm thankful that the nurses who cared for my newborn babies and the doctor who did my dad's heart surgery didn't just read how-tos in a book and pass written tests but had years of experience before it was time to actually put into practice what they were trained to do.

HEAD KNOWLEDGE IS NOT ENOUGH

I fear many Christian parents today are filling their children's heads with knowledge from the Word but not giving them any hands-on experience in applying what they've learned. In the same way that it's not enough to have the driver's education manual memorized, it's not enough for kids to have the Bible memorized. They must live it out. They must become doers of the Word.

> But don't just listen to God's word. You must do what it says. Otherwise, you are only fooling yourselves. For if you listen to the word and don't obey, it is like glancing at your face in a mirror. You see yourself, walk away, and forget what you look like. But if you look carefully into the perfect law that sets you free, and if you do what it says and don't forget what you heard, then God will bless you for doing it.
> —JAMES 1:22–25

James was onto something that educators all over the world know to be true—there are many benefits associated with hands-on training.

One source found that when students were given the opportunity to practice what they learned, the percentage of what they retained jumped from 20 percent to 75 percent.[2] Students in a practical, hands-on environment are very often engaged, stimulated, and eager to learn as much as possible. They are also more empowered to direct their own learning, and their critical-thinking skills increase because they must make decisions on what to do next to receive the outcome they are striving to obtain. These critical-thinking skills remain with the student, in contrast to the material they simply memorize for a test and then forget after the exam. Students who learn in a hands-on environment typically have an instructor nearby with real-world experience and knowledge who can help them if they have difficulty with a task they are trying to complete. The expert advice can help them perform the task correctly and safely as they may one day be required to do in their workplace.

You can talk to your kids about being salt, light, and love every day. You can encourage them to memorize Scripture, highlight verses in their Bibles, and recite the confessions in this book every night before bed—but if they aren't doers of the Word, they're fooling themselves and you're wasting your time. Why? *Because what is in their heads can move to their hearts only through hands-on experience!*

Our kids must "get behind the wheel" so they can experience what it's like to walk in the plans and purposes God has for them. They're going to need a trusty, experienced instructor to sit next to them, guide them, and tap the emergency brakes if needed. Are you up for the job?

Now, I am not going to offer you a step-by-step

guide on how to move your kids from hearers to doers here, because God's plan for my family is unique and God's plan for your family is unique. But I am going to give you some insight into what has worked with our kids. It's a process that is always changing and one in which we have to let the Holy Spirit lead the way, but I trust that as you read about some of our hands-on moments, God will begin to speak specifically to you about the plans He has for your children.

Remember, you didn't fashion your arrows to look pretty. You fashioned them to be sent out to *do* something—to do what you've been training them to do. To help you hit the target, I've put together some goals and broken them down into daily, weekly, monthly, and yearly real-life activities.

GOALS FOR BEING SALT, LIGHT, AND LOVE

I'm a big believer in the power of a calendar. What we write on our calendars, we *do*. If you have a dentist appointment written down on your calendar for 2:00 p.m. this Thursday, guess where you are going to be at 2:00 p.m. this Thursday. At the dentist's office, of course! I want to challenge you with a statement I once heard at a conference that changed our family forever: My calendar is not just about what I have to get done, but about who I want to *become*.

So if you desire for your family to become a family that is *doing* the Word, get out your calendar and write down what the Holy Spirit reveals to you.

177

DAILY

I have fifteen minutes in the car with my children every morning before school, and I have chosen to use that fifteen minutes to disciple them. As soon as we pull out of our garage, we begin talking about a verse we're learning together, or I share with them something cool God showed me during my quiet time. I pray over them and often have one of them pray. We talk about what we're expecting God to do because God is looking for those who are waiting for Him to move in their lives. I remind them they are called to be salt, light, and love to the people God puts on their paths that day, and then we pray a six-word prayer—a prayer that we should all pray every day: *Thank You. Fill me. Use me.*

Thank You. My kids know that the password to God's presence is "thank You," and because we want to start our day in His presence, where there is fullness of joy, we begin by saying, "Thank You." We enter His gates with thanksgiving in our hearts and go into His courts with praise. (See Psalm 100:4.) No matter what is going on in our lives, we always have something to be thankful for.

Fill me. We also want the fullness of God released in our lives every day, so each morning we ask Jesus to fill us afresh with His Spirit. We'll take all the help, power, and comfort we can get! (See John 16:7–15 and Acts 1:8.)

Use me. Finally, we make ourselves available to be used by God in whatever way He chooses to use us.

We desire to be like Isaiah. We want to be the answer to God's question when He asks, "Who will go for Me?" "Here we are," we say. "Send us!" (See Isaiah 6:8.)

I remind my children every day to be looking and listening for opportunities to be used by God. Often we think we have to send our children to a third-world country for them to make a difference, but I believe they can make a more significant impact at their school lunch tables than they can on a weeklong mission trip to Peru spent performing a Christian dance skit every day and handing out tracts.

Don't get me wrong: Mission trips are great. But if our children don't know how to reach the kids at their schools, what are we doing sending them across the world to try to reach people they have zero connection with? *We need to teach our children that God wants to use them on regular days in regular ways.* It's not always about attending "See You at the Pole" events or starting Christians on Campus Clubs. It's teaching them to go through their daily lives open and available to be used by God—in big or small ways. It's encouraging them to have the attitude that says, "Send me."

It's important for our kids to know that being used by God doesn't have to be weird or spooky. I tell my kids all the time to be looking for people who seem sad, discouraged, or lonely and to notice when friends or teachers are having a rough day, week, or year. When the Holy Spirit highlights those people to our children, they have a decision to make. Are they going to be doers or just hearers only? Are they

179

actually going to let their light shine? Are they going to respond in love? Are they going to share a verse or invite the people to church? Will they sit next to the kid on the bus whom no one else sits by because God asked them to? Will they include someone because God asked them to? Will they tell their friends the truth when they see them making wrong decisions? Will their actions help someone taste and see that the Lord is good?

On the way home from school I ask my kids if they had any salt, light, or love moments. Whom did you encourage? Whom did you serve? Whom did you include? Whose day did you brighten? Whom did you stand up for? I love when they have a moment to share. The excitement in their voices, the spark in their eyes, and the joy in their smiles all tell me they're learning that nothing compares to being used by God.

Sometimes at dinner I like to give my kids a particular scenario and then ask them how they think Jesus would act in that scenario. This is an important exercise because the Bible tells us it is our destiny to think like Jesus, act like Jesus, talk like Jesus, serve like Jesus, and love like Jesus. (See 2 Corinthians 3:18.) Here's an example:

"Let's say all the kids in class are planning a mean prank on a teacher. Imagine that Jesus walks by and hears about the prank. Remember all the stories you have heard about Jesus, and then tell me what you think He would do."

I let them think for a little while and then share their ideas. After they share, I remind them that how they think Jesus would act is exactly how they should act if they ever find themselves in a similar situation. They can't just *talk about* being salt, light, and love; they have to *be* salt, light, and love.

Disclaimer: A lot of days my kids get caught up in their tasks and miss opportunities to be salt, light, and love, just as I do. They don't have moments to share every day. But God's mercies are new every morning, and His grace is enough for us. We may miss assignments, but He's faithful to give us new ones if we are faithful to ask. So let's all keep praying that six-word prayer: *Thank You. Fill me. Use me.*

WEEKLY

Every Sunday our kids serve in a ministry at our church called Titus 2. It's an incredible program that instills a heart for serving in the local church in elementary-aged children. We want our children to know that church isn't a place where you go and consume; it is a place you go and contribute. There is no better place for a child to discover and develop their gifts than the local church. My ten-year-old son, Gus, serves in the nursery each Sunday. He rocks babies, feeds them their bottles, lies down on the floor next to them, and entertains them while their parents attend church. My eight-year-old daughter, Beau, serves in the two-year-old class. She builds towers out of Magna-Tiles® and mans the train table as if it's her job! She sings and does all the motions during praise and worship to model what worship looks like for the little ones. She helps pass out snacks and serves the teachers in whatever ways she can.

Gus and Beau both love what they do! It's wonderful for them to be a small part of something that's much bigger than they are and to know they are serving God in the process. Working with little ones as they do is an incredible hands-on experience—the type that I believe keeps people planted in church and their families flourishing. If you don't know what that's like, waste no time in joining a serve team at your church—and signing your children up too!

In our self-centered and selfie-oriented world it's vital that we involve our children in actives in which they must serve people who can do nothing for them in return. If your church doesn't have a serve team for kids, maybe God is calling you to pioneer one. But no matter where or what it is, find something your kids can do on a weekly basis that involves being salt, light, and love.

MONTHLY

Every month a small amount is withdrawn from our checking account to help support a five-year-old boy named Walter. Walter lives in extreme poverty right in our own backyard—Arkansas. For less than two dollars a day we're able to partner with an organization that provides Walter with medical care, educational support, life skills, and job training before graduation. We exchange letters and photos with Walter and let him know he's loved by our family of five in Oklahoma City.

We have involved our children in this process since Day 1. They helped us choose Walter, and they are the ones who write most of the letters. We pray for him together, and we plan on meeting him someday soon.

This is just one way we let our lives fulfill God's Word. If there is a canned food drive at school—we bring cans. If there is an Angel Tree at church—we bring gifts. We are always on the lookout for opportunities to be generous, and we make sure to include our children in whatever we're up to.

YEARLY

For the last three years Josh and I have spent New Year's Eve with our kids. During the time together we play games, eat tons of junk food, and when the clock strikes 10 p.m. (we can't hang till midnight anymore), we ring in the new year with kisses and hope-filled hugs. But before we break out Monopoly and the pizza rolls we all regret the next day, we spend time writing down our goals.

The five of us gather and map out some family goals. Our family goals in the past have included saving up enough money to take a Disneyland vacation, spending more time with grandparents, playing outside more, and making healthier eating choices (after the New Year's Eve party, of course).

And then we ask the kids to share their personal goals. It's always tough for them to get going at first, but after a while they begin rapid-firing them, and I have a difficult time keeping up: "Read x amount of books this year." "Make this sports team." "Get along better with my sister." "Learn how to do a cartwheel." "Audition for the talent show."

Those are all great goals, but I have learned that if we want to keep them focused on their eternal purpose, their goal list also has to include actions that line up with that purpose. How can they shine more light this year? How can they help more people taste that the Lord is good? How can they be more loving? I let them come up with their own goals that correspond to being salt and light and loving God and others, and then I help them accomplish those goals.

Maybe your son wants to bring five friends to church in the upcoming year. Don't just write that goal down on paper and hope for the best. What steps need to be taken to make sure that it is actually accomplished? Do you need to plan a play date? Do you need to show up at class parties so you can meet the parents of the friends your child wants to invite? Do you need to exchange phone numbers or send an invitation to a special church service via email or Facebook?

Maybe your daughter desires to raise money for a family in need. What does that look like? Help her come up with a plan. Could she hold a garage sale, set up a lemonade stand, or start a babysitting business? Or perhaps your child desires to take ownership of his relationship with God. He is ready to start reading God's Word on his own. Take him to a bookstore, let him pick out a daily devotional designed for kids and a Bible, and help him decide when would be a great time to read them each day.

BECOMING LIVING MESSAGES

Whatever godly goals your children set, remember: *Don't just make lists; think through steps, put dates on the calendar, and assist your children in whatever ways you can to help them be doers of the Word.* Otherwise you run the risk of fitting the apostle James' description of someone who talks the talk but doesn't walk the walk:

> Anyone who sets himself up as "religious" by talking a good game is self-deceived. This kind of religion is hot air and only hot air. Real religion, the kind that passes muster before God the Father, is this: Reach out to the homeless and loveless in their plight, and guard against corruption from the godless world.
>
> —JAMES 1:26–27, MSG

Let his description smack you upside the head—in a good way. A way that snaps you out of your complacency and gets you off the couch. A way that causes you to spring into action. A way that keeps you from being a religious hot-air bag and causes you to move from being a hearer only to a legitimate doer. A way that helps you practice what James calls "real religion."

I know I don't want people to think of our family when they read the first two sentences in that passage. Isaiah 8:18 is the verse I want my family associated with: "Here I am with the children the Lord has given me. The Lord Almighty, whose throne is on Mount

Zion, has sent us as living messages to the people of Israel" (GNT).

Isaiah had two sons, Maher-shalal-hash-baz and Shear-jashub. (See Isaiah 8:1–4; 7:3.) Their names were prophetic messages to Israel. Maher-shalal-hash-baz was a walking billboard that read, in essence, "Speed to the spoil; hurry to the plunder," which spoke of a coming attack by Assyria.[3] Shear-jashub's billboard read, "A remnant shall return," which referred to the restoration that God would bring.[4] And Isaiah's name meant "Jehovah has saved."[5] God sent Isaiah and his two sons as living messages to the people—they were signs, symbols, proof, reminders, and object lessons pointing people to the coming Christ.

God has sent my family to be living messages. He has sent your family to be living messages. The key word here is *living*. The lives we are living should be signs, symbols, proof, reminders, and object lessons that point people to Jesus. Don't worry; you don't have to change your name or the name of any of your children to fulfill this call! You can be walking billboards and continue to go by the names you've always gone by. But ask yourself, What message are my children and I putting out there?

Many families don't see themselves as living messages and therefore aren't seeking hands-on experiences, but Jesus said of us, with reference to Isaiah 8:17–18 (NIV), "I will put my trust in him," that is, "I and the children God has given me" (Heb. 2:13).

Jesus—Immanuel—Christ with us—is with us, His children. He stands with us as Isaiah stood with his children, and He wants you to know today that there are people in your sphere of influence who have never opened their Bibles but who are getting to know Him because they are getting to know your family. Don't take this lightly.

Today, you choose. Will your family be religious hot-air bags or life-saving, hope-giving, living messages who are doers of the Word?

QUESTIONS FOR DISCUSSION

1. Share about a time when biblical head knowledge became heart knowledge for you because of hands-on experience.

2. What are some ideas that come to mind when you think about daily, weekly, and monthly activities your family can engage in to move from being hearers to being doers of the Word?

3. Which part of the six-word prayer comes naturally to your family—thankfulness, Spirit-filled living, or being used by God? Have you been neglecting any of these areas?

4. Did you have any yearly family goals last year? What are some goals you want to work toward in the coming year? How do they correlate to being salt, light, and love?

5. If we are living messages—walking billboards—what message do you believe your billboard displays? What do you want people to think when they think about your family?

PRAYER FOR PARENTS

Lord, here I am with my children, living messages. We are signs, symbols, proof, reminders, and object lessons that point people to Jesus. Thank You for standing with me. Thank You for reminding me how crucial it is to be a doer of the Word. Lord, give me Spirit-led ideas and help me provide unforgettable, hands-on learning experiences for my children. May all the biblical head knowledge they gain find a place in their hearts as they live it out. Give me wisdom and special insight as I choose to ride in the passenger seat and train my children to be salt, light, and love. In Jesus' name, amen.

CONFESSION FOR CHILDREN

Thank You! I purpose to be the owner of a thankful heart. No matter what I am going through, there is always something to be thankful for. Thanksgiving daily leads me into God's presence. I desire to be near God's heart. I am filled with the Spirit of God. I want all of Him I can get. The Holy Spirit helps me, empowers me, emboldens me, and guides me throughout the day. I offer my hands, my feet, my eyes, my smile, and my voice to the service of God. I expect to be used by Him today. I see opportunities in which I can partner with God to see His will carried out on earth as it is in heaven. I am a doer of the Word. I am a living message.

Chapter 12

GREATER IS HE WHO IS IN YOU

I N CHAPTER 1 you read that our number one goal in parenting is to help our children daily experience Jesus and all His goodness so they follow Him willingly instead of walking in darkness. I truly believe that if we present an irresistible Jesus to our kids, they will surrender their lives to Him without a fight. But until they do, all I have taught you to do with your kids will be for naught. They may comply with what you tell them, but their hearts won't be in it. The Bible tells us that "people who aren't spiritual can't receive these truths from God's Spirit. It all sounds foolish to them and they can't understand it, for only those who are spiritual can understand what the Spirit means" (1 Cor. 2:14).

So let me ask you: Have your children surrendered their lives to Jesus? Have they been born again?

If not, has the gospel message been presented to them in such a way that they can grasp what Jesus did for them on the cross? If so, do they know how to live a life here on earth that honors His sacrifice as they wait to spend eternity in heaven? Do they understand what it means to die to self—to let God's Spirit lead them instead of their flesh? Do they realize that they *have been* made perfect but *are being* made holy? Perfection in the sight of God happens immediately, but transforming into the image of Jesus is an ongoing process. They must know they will make mistakes and sin along the way but that Jesus has paid the price for every one of their sins—past, present, and future.

It's important for your children to know that saying a prayer to invite Jesus into their lives is just the beginning of new life in Christ. It's the first step. In order to grow and mature in the things of God, they will want to take the additional steps of being water baptized; asking Jesus to fill them with His Spirit; learning all they can about Jesus through His Word so they can become like Him; and being salt, light, and love to the world around them.

It's also vital for them to understand that saying a prayer and believing in their hearts doesn't only save them from hell and reserve a spot for them in heaven; salvation enables them to have a relationship with God. We must help them to acknowledge the sin gap that separated them from being able to walk and talk with their Father and to see Jesus as the bridge that closed that gap and made a way for them to have a very real friendship with God—a friendship God deeply desires to have with them.

If your children are not already born again, they can be. And I can't think of a better person to lead them to salvation than you, mighty warrior. Josh and I led our older son and daughter to the Lord, and our younger daughter is nearing the age at which we feel we can present the gospel to her and invite her to make Jesus her Lord and Savior. We want her to truly understand what the decision means because it is on a different level from deciding which tutu she wants to wear to ballet class. This is the most important decision she will ever make, and it's one she must choose to make again day after day after day.

On that glorious day we will present her with a spiritual birth certificate, as we did for the older two. The certificate will be signed and dated by Mom and Dad—proof that just as we got to witness her first birth, we got to witness her miraculous second birth. We want her always to remember which day in history she decided to follow Jesus. She'll also receive a big-girl Bible with her name on it. And every year after that, on her spiritual birthday, we will celebrate with cupcakes, candles, and a small gift. The heavens celebrate, so why shouldn't we?

After she receives salvation, we will talk with her about the Holy Spirit and ask her if she would like to be filled with the Holy Spirit. And because Jesus is no respecter of persons, if she says yes, she will be legitimately saved and filled.

VICTORY OVER THE ANTICHRIST

In the appendix you'll find a guide that will help you as you lead your children to receive the greatest gifts of all time—salvation and the baptism in the Holy Spirit. Once the miracle of salvation takes place in your child's life, you can be sure that the following promise, and every other promise pertaining to God's children, applies to them:

> Little children, you are of God [you belong to Him] and have [already] defeated and overcome them [the agents of the antichrist], because He Who lives in you is greater (mightier) than he who is in the world.
>
> —1 JOHN 4:4, AMPC

Why is it important that your children have already defeated and overcome the agents of the Antichrist? Because according to pastor, Bible teacher, and Bible commentator David Guzik, the spirit of the Antichrist "is the spirit which both *opposes* the true Jesus and offers a *substitute* Jesus."[1]

Jesus came to bring peace, joy, and hope, but the agents of the Antichrist bring stress, depression, and hopelessness. Jesus came to set us free, but the agents of the Antichrist work to enslave people with addictions such as pornography, drugs, alcohol, social media, approval, sex, eating, gambling, and more. Jesus came to heal the brokenhearted, but the agents of the Antichrist delight in breaking hearts.

The spirit of the Antichrist is active in our world right now. It is busy opposing all we have come to know about Jesus through His Word and by His Spirit. It is offering substitutes that wreck people's lives both here on earth and for eternity. It is active in our cities, our neighborhoods, and our children's schools.

But don't fret. Remember what 1 John 4:4 says? "You are of God"—and your born-again children are of God as well. You belong to God, and your born-again children belong to God. Because Jesus, who is greater than the antichrist spirit that is active in this world, lives in you and in your born-again children, your family has already defeated and overcome Satan and all his allies. *Greater is He who is in your children than he who is in the world.*

You either believe that or you don't. If you don't, perhaps you don't believe your children are truly saved. Hear me: You must activate your faith! We are saved by grace through faith. Romans 10:9 confirms this truth: "If you confess with your mouth that Jesus is Lord and believe in your heart that God raised him from the dead, you will be saved" (ESV).

If your children have confessed and believed just as this verse says, they are saved. They believe it! Now you must believe it with them so you can take them by the hands and start teaching them about their new lives in Christ. If you fail to see your children as children of God, belonging to Him instead of belonging to you, you'll miss out on the opportunity to partner with the Holy Spirit to raise godly kids in this ungodly world. Worse, you'll upset Jesus.

LET THE LITTLE CHILDREN COME TO ME...

There are three occasions recorded in Scripture on which Jesus got upset. The first and most famous of these is described in Matthew 21:12–13—the time when Jesus drove the money changers out of the temple. In this case Jesus was mad because they turned God's house into a marketplace, where they cheated and took advantage of people who were there to worship.

The second occasion is found in Mark 3:1–5, which tells us that Jesus singled out a man in the synagogue who had a shriveled hand, undoubtedly with the intent of healing him, and the people got upset because it was the Sabbath. How did Jesus respond? He "looked around at them in anger and, deeply distressed at their stubborn hearts, said to the man, 'Stretch out your hand'" (v. 5, NIV). They did not prevent Him from doing what He was called to do and healing the man, but He was angered by their legalistic view that it was wrong to do anything—even something good—on the holy day.

The third occasion stands alone as the only place in Scripture that records Jesus' getting upset with His own people. Let me set the stage. At one point the disciples came to Jesus and asked Him who is the greatest in the kingdom of heaven. (See Matthew 18:1.) In response He called a child to Him and set the child in the midst of them. Then He said, "Assuredly, I say to you, unless you are converted and become as little children, you will by no means enter the kingdom of heaven. Therefore whoever humbles himself as this little child is the greatest in the kingdom of heaven. Whoever receives one little child like this in My name receives Me" (Matt. 18:2–5, NKJV).

After that I'm sure the word on the street was, "Jesus loves the little children." Parents and grandparents who heard the word wanted to bring their children to Him—but the disciples weren't happy about it. "Then little children were brought to Jesus, that He might put His hands on them and pray; but the disciples rebuked those who brought them" (Matt. 19:13, AMPC). They had a lot of nerve, considering that Jesus had just given them an object lesson about becoming like children and receiving little children in His name!

Understandably, Jesus didn't let them get away with it. The Bible says He was "indignant" when He saw what the disciples were doing (Mark 10:14, NIV). So He said to them, "Let the little children come to me, and do not hinder them, for the kingdom of heaven belongs to such as these" (Matt. 19:14, NIV).

I love the first part of that response: "Let the little children come to me." That tells us children *wanted* to come to Jesus. They were trying to get to Him. Why? The Bible doesn't say exactly, but I think it's because kids are excellent judges of character. They knew this Man was kind, loving, and fun. They wanted to get close to Him. They must have felt they could trust Him, because it's not like a child to want to go talk to someone they don't feel is welcoming. And I'm sure the children were a breath of fresh air to Jesus after dealing with Pharisees and disciples who didn't always get Him.

... AND DO NOT HINDER THEM

The word *hinder* in Matthew 19:14 comes from the Greek word *kōlyō*, which means to forbid, prevent, restrain, keep from, or withhold.[2] The disciples were literally standing in the way of these children's approaching Jesus.

Surely believing parents wouldn't prevent their children from coming to Jesus, would we? Hopefully not. But the word *hinder* also means "to withhold." Though I don't believe parents deliberately stand in the way of their children's coming to Jesus, I do think those who are not actively looking for ways to provide their kids with opportunities to be in His presence and to connect with His Word are withholding Jesus from them. Children need the Christian adults in their lives to provide them with ways to receive ministry from Him.

Children are not too young or too silly to have a life-giving relationship with Jesus, but if we aren't purposeful in bringing them to Him, they might miss out on the life God has planned for them. The word on the street is the same today as it was two thousand years ago—Jesus loves the little children. So do whatever you can to make sure Jesus is not being withheld from the children in your life. Don't hinder the little ones who mean so much to the Lord!

In the same way that you were diligent to teach your sons and daughters to correctly recite the alphabet, to sneeze into their elbows, to tie their shoes, and that the word *hippopotamus* contains five syllables, you must be diligent to teach them important truths such as greater is the One living in them than the one living in the world. That's difficult to do if you don't believe your children are truly saved and that God's promises apply to them just as they apply to you. Start agreeing with God's Word and stop agreeing with the fears you have about losing your children to the world. Let your children come to Jesus—don't hinder them by your unbelief.

FOLLOW ME AS I FOLLOW CHRIST

If your children have been born again, they have access to a constant supply of God's Spirit inside them. The same Spirit that raised Christ from the dead—not one kind of like it, not one similar to it, but the *exact same Spirit* that is responsible for the resurrection of Jesus— is alive in your children, which means they can win every single day. They can *more* than conquer temptation, sin, setbacks, doubt, anxiety, rejection, shame, and literally any other thing that the enemy has up his sleeve. But—and this is a *big* but—you must believe it. Once you believe it, you can begin to teach your children to lean into and rely on the Greater One who is alive in them. One of the best ways you can teach your children to rely on God's Spirit is for you to live out your reliance on Him in front of them.

Our children must witness our desperation, hunger, and thirst for God. They must know we are entirely dependent on Him. They must see us on our knees and in the Word. They must observe our worshipping God on the mountaintops, and they must especially observe our worshipping Him in the valleys. They must sense our desire to be used by God and the joy we possess as we serve in His kingdom.

Children are always watching their parents. Do yours see you seeking Him first and walking in the victory that has already been won for you, or do they see you being overwhelmed by the spirit of the Antichrist?

The apostle Paul told the people of the church at Corinth, "Pattern yourselves after me [follow my example], as I imitate and follow Christ (the Messiah)" (1 Cor. 11:1, AMPC). He encouraged them to imitate him as he was imitating Jesus. He knew they needed an example, and he was more than happy to be one for them. He knew if they studied his mannerisms, his expressions, the way he talked, the way he worshipped, and the way he treated other people, they would start to pattern their lives after him and essentially be patterning their lives after Jesus.

What if we lived our lives in such a way—privately and publicly—that we could say with complete confidence to our children, "Pattern yourselves after me (follow my example), as I imitate and follow Christ"?

You may not have your own television show or fifty thousand Instagram followers, but you do have your own audience. I have three little fans who watch me every single day for hours at a time. They are patterning themselves after me, following my example, and if I'm patterning myself after Jesus, that means they are too!

Mighty warrior, God has not given you a spirit of fear. He has given you power, love, and a sound mind. You have everything you need to be a fearless parent. You have everything you need to sharpen your arrowheads, shoot them down the straight and narrow path, and watch them soar into the good future that God designed for them. You have everything you need to map out your children's God-given purpose to love God and to love others as the salt of the earth and the light of the world. You have everything you need to stand with your children as living messages of the goodness of God. You have everything you need to raise your children in this upside-down world *in faith*. Why? Because you belong to God and therefore have already conquered. The One living in you is far greater than the one who is in the world. Don't hinder your children or withhold Jesus from them; bring them to Him!

It's time for you to take up the mantle of Jochebed. Be the parent who sees God-given purpose in your children from a young age. Be the parent who is not afraid of the culture of the world. Be the parent who does not allow fear to author your children's stories. Be the parent who takes advantage of every opportunity to instill God's Word in your children. Be the parent who raises some of the greatest leaders the world has ever seen. Be the parent whose children light their torches at your flame.

QUESTIONS FOR DISCUSSION

1. Do you believe your children are truly born again? If so, share about their decision to follow Jesus. If not, do you sense they are ready to hear the gospel message and make the decision to surrender their lives to Jesus, making Him the Lord and Savior of their lives?

2. At what point did you realize that salvation was more than a reserved spot in heaven and an escape from hell? When did your relationship with Jesus begin?

3. What do you think is the greatest hang-up in believing that we belong to God and that Jesus in us is greater than the spirit of the Antichrist in the world?

4. We want our children to imitate us as we imitate Jesus. In what areas of your life are you best imitating Jesus? Are there any areas of your life in which you want to emulate Jesus more closely?

5. What have been your greatest takeaways from this book? How has it changed the way you will parent moving forward?

PRAYER FOR PARENTS

Lord, help me to remember that my born-again children belong to You! Every promise in Scripture applies to them. I desire to continually set them in Your midst—to make a way for them to come to You. Thank You for opening my eyes to see that my children are not too young to know You and have a real relationship with You. Right now, I commit to start agreeing with God's Word and stop agreeing with any fears I have about losing my children to the world. I believe that the same Spirit that raised Christ from the dead is alive in my children. Help me to teach them to rely on the Holy Spirit. May they see me reliant upon You. May they see me hunger and thirst for You and You alone. I want to say to my children with confidence, "Pattern yourselves after me." Thank You, God, for giving me everything I need to be a fearless parent. I take up the mantle of Jochebed in Jesus' name. Amen.

CONFESSION FOR CHILDREN

I am a child of God. I belong to Him. I have already defeated and overcome the stress, depression, and hopelessness brought about by the agents of the Antichrist. Greater is Christ in me than the evil in this world.

Jesus loves me and wants me to spend time with

Him. I don't have to wait until I am an adult to have a real friendship with Jesus. I won't let anyone or anything keep me from Him. The same Spirit that raised Christ from the dead is alive in me! I can more than conquer temptation, sin, setbacks, rejection, shame, and *anything* the enemy tries to use to take me down. I will follow after Jesus, and I will not walk in darkness.

Appendix

HOW TO LEAD YOUR CHILDREN TO CHRIST

L EADING YOUR CHILDREN to Christ is one of the most significant things you can do as a parent. In this appendix you'll find some helpful questions to pose to your children as you prepare to lead them to receive the gift of eternal salvation through Jesus and the infilling of the Holy Spirit. You may be wondering what age is the right age to lead your children to Christ—there is no right age. It's more about the readiness of each child's heart and their ability to comprehend the weight of their decision than it is about how many candles were on their last birthday cake.

Pre-Salvation Prayer Questions

Your children need to understand several key truths in order to put their faith in Jesus. They need to realize they need a Savior, and they need to understand the importance of Jesus' death and resurrection and what it means to live for Jesus. To ensure your children grasp those concepts, you can open a discussion about salvation by asking some or all of the following questions.

1. Do you believe that Jesus died on the cross?

You can use Romans 5:8, Matthew 27, Mark 15, Luke 23, and/or John 19 to show your children what the Bible says about Jesus' death on the cross.

2. Why did Jesus have to die on the cross?

If your children are unable to explain the necessity of the cross, you can talk to them about sin separation. Here is a brief outline you can follow:

> Did you know that before Jesus died on the cross, there was a big gap called "sin" that separated God's people from Him? [See John 14:6 and 1 Peter 3:18.] Sin is when we miss the mark God has for us. Here's an example of sin: God has commanded us to love our neighbors as we love ourselves. If we lie, cheat, or steal from our neighbor, we miss the mark. Can you think of a time when you have sinned? [Parents, consider sharing an age-appropriate time when you sinned.]
>
> We *all* sin [Rom. 3:23], and our sin separates us from God. That breaks God's heart because He wants to be near us! We are His family! He knew He needed to give us a way to get sin out of our lives and to bridge the gap between us and Him, and He decided that Jesus would be that

bridge! [See 2 Corinthians 5:21 and Philippians 3:8–9.]

Jesus came to the earth as a little baby in the manger. He never sinned, not even once, and when He was thirty-three years old, He died on the cross. When He died, His blood spilled out, and His blood is the very thing God needed to wash away our sins. If Jesus hadn't given His life for us on the cross, our sin would have separated us from God forever. [See Ephesians 1:7 and Hebrews 9:14, 22.]

3. Do you believe that Jesus rose again after dying on the cross?

See Matthew 28:5–6 and Romans 10:9–10 for help discussing the fact that Jesus not only died on the cross but also rose again after being in the tomb for three days. Make sure your children understand that Jesus' resurrection was the sign that He won the victory over sin. It also proved that God was pleased with Jesus' sacrifice on the cross and that it was enough to wash away our sins so they would no longer separate us from God.

4. What do you think it looks like to give your whole life to Jesus?

It's important for your children to grasp that salvation is not a decision that only affects where they will spend eternity; it's also meant to affect each day they spend here on earth for the rest of their lives. Tell your children that giving Jesus their life means they are deciding to follow Him and His ways. You can say,

"Giving your life to Jesus is saying He is the King of your heart! You will no longer be the boss of your life; instead you are giving Jesus control." Consider using Matthew 6:33 and Matthew 22:37 to discuss with your children the importance of giving God their whole heart.

5. Did you know that today if you say with your mouth that Jesus is Lord and believe in your heart that God raised Him from the dead, you are welcomed into the family of God?

You can tell your children the following:

> Romans 10:9–10 says if you say with your mouth that Jesus is Lord and believe in your heart that God raised Him from the dead, you will live with Jesus in heaven forever. God will be your Father. Jesus will be your Brother. And the Holy Spirit will be your Friend. Mom will be your sister in Christ, and Dad will be your brother in Christ! You won't just be part of this family; you will be part of the family of God!

6. Do you want to give your whole life to Jesus?

If your children answer yes, lead them in the salvation prayer by having them repeat the following, or something similar, after you.

> *Dear God, I say with my mouth that Jesus is Lord. Jesus is my Lord and my Savior. I believe with all my heart that Jesus died and that You raised Him from the dead. His blood has washed away all my past and*

future sins. I'm sorry for my sins. But now
sin no longer separates me from You. Thank
You for forgiving me. I give You my life. Thank
You for giving me a brand-new, perfect spirit!
Thank You for welcoming me into the family
of God. In Jesus' name, amen.

Never force your children to pray this prayer. If they are not ready to commit their lives to Jesus, do not be shocked, appalled, or angry. This is a decision they have to make on their own and in their own time. If you are unsure as to why they do not want to make Jesus Lord of their lives, simply ask them to help you understand. Respect their decision, answer their questions, and continue to pray for them. Pray that God's kingdom would come and that His will would be done in their life.

After Your Children Say Amen

Celebrate! Hug, laugh, cry, have cake, and rejoice! After all, this is the greatest and most significant moment of their lives. Let them know how proud you are of them, how happy Jesus is to begin a relationship with them, and that the angels in heaven are celebrating too!

Post-Salvation Questions

After your children have accepted Christ, use the following questions to ensure they understand what happens next.

1. Did you know that you are made up of three parts?

You can tell your child the following:

> You are a spirit. Your spirit lives in your body. And you have a mind—that's where your thoughts and feelings come from. [See 1 Thessalonians 5:23.]
>
> Just now, when you prayed, something incredible happened to your spirit! Your spirit was made *new*. Your old spirit died, and a new spirit was born. And the new spirit that was born is perfect. You get a fresh start, and all of your sins are washed away. [See 2 Corinthians 5:17–20.] Your new spirit can never die. When your body dies, your spirit is what goes to heaven! [See John 3:16.]
>
> But what about your body? Does it look new? No, you didn't get a new body. You'll get a new body in heaven.
>
> What about your mind? Do you feel different? Does it seem like you have different thoughts?
>
> No, you didn't get a new mind. Your spirit is perfect right now, but your mind and body are *being made* perfect. [See Hebrews 10:14.] In other words, you will still make mistakes even though your spirit is new, but the blood of Jesus has washed away every sin—all your past sins and every sin you will ever commit in the future. We don't have to live a perfect life to get into heaven, because Jesus lived a perfect life for us. [See Ephesians 2:8–9.] He made your spirit

perfect forever. You can't mess up His perfect gift of a perfect spirit!

2. Do you think that because Jesus has taken care of all our future sins, we should sin whenever we want and do whatever we want?

You can share with your child the following:

Jesus gave His life to free us from sin. Sin slows us down, hurts us, and stops us from living the way God wants us to live. Just because Jesus has already washed away our future sins doesn't mean we have a license to sin. We should not fall back into a trap Jesus paid for us to get out of. Having the blood of Jesus covering our sins means we get to live a life that honors God every day in every way. [See 1 Peter 4:1–2.] When you do sin, tell God you're sorry that you hurt His heart, and He will help you move on. [See 1 John 1:8–10.]

3. Since you received a brand-new spirit, what kind of things do you think would help your spirit grow?

Give your children some helpful hints:

Here are a few ideas: Read the Bible to make your thoughts new, go to church, and spend time talking to God each day through prayer. Just like a new baby needs food to grow, your new spirit needs food! [See Matthew 4:4; Romans 12:2; 1 Thessalonians 5:17; 1 Timothy 4:7; Hebrews 10:25; and James 5:16.]

LEADING YOUR CHILD TO RECEIVE THE BAPTISM IN THE HOLY SPIRIT

The Holy Spirit is for kids too! Use the following questions to lead your children in understanding how the Holy Spirit helps us and how to receive the baptism in the Holy Spirit.

1. Do you think it might be hard to keep from sinning?

2. Would you like Jesus to walk with you and help you every day?

3. Did you know that before Jesus went to heaven, He told His disciples that He was sending a Helper for us?

Tell your children the following:

> Jesus promised the Holy Spirit—a helper who could live inside every person with a new spirit. He is someone who could help us obey, teach us things about the Bible, comfort us, and let us know when we are on the right track or when we are on the wrong track. Jesus wants you to have the Holy Spirit living inside you to be your Helper every single day. He also will give you the boldness to resist temptation to sin, and to tell others about Jesus. [See John 14:15–27 to discuss with your child what the Holy Spirit does for us.]

211

4. Would you like the Holy Spirit to be your Helper?

If he or she says yes, have your child repeat the following prayer after you:

Jesus, I ask You to fill me with the Holy Spirit to help me obey You and to do Your will for the rest of my life. In Your name I pray. Amen.

If you would like to go further and teach your children about the gifts the Holy Spirit gives, read 1 Corinthians 12.

Lastly, children hear what you say, but they believe what you do. As you are one of the greatest influencers in your child's life, may they see you taking up your cross and living a life that honors God in every area!

ACKNOWLEDGMENTS

Writing a book has been a dream of mine since I was nine years old. I still remember my third-grade teacher, Mrs. Day, telling me I was a gifted writer. She may have just been being kind, but I bought it. I became very interested in writing, and because I was interested, my parents took an interest. They sent me to a young author's conference and took me to meet local children's authors in the area. My mom helped me illustrate my books. Eventually I outgrew my author phase and became more interested in cheerleading, boys, and youth group—but just as they supported me in my quest to be an author, my parents supported me through every cheerleading tryout, tumbling lesson, football game, mission trip—and any and everything else I showed an interest in. They kept me grounded yet made me believe I could do all things through Christ. Thank you, Mom and Dad, for seeing greatness in me and calling it out of me.

To my husband. My closest friend and loudest cheerleader—to the ends of the earth I would follow you. You dream big and challenge my faith in the best possible way. Thank you for helping me pace myself throughout this process. You love me so good. There is no one I'd rather have by my side as we purpose to raise godly kids who make a difference. You know.

To Ken and Trudi, a.k.a. Nana and Papa. Thank you for being the greatest in-laws on the face of the earth. Thanks for giving me a chance and allowing me to help write curriculum for your ministry all those years ago. Working for Ken Blount Ministries sparked my love for writing again. Thank you for praying for me, being there for me through thick and thin, and building a godly legacy that we are honored to carry on.

I'm forever grateful for friends like Heather Lane, who faithfully sent me a text message every Monday morning while I was writing this book to let me know she was praying for me; Aubrey Oaks, who loved this book as if it were her own and convinced me the advertising part would be as much fun as the writing; and Courtney Haggard, Afton Filkins, and Christen Romano, who locked arms with me and prayed over things concerning the book that we saw God answer in mighty ways!

To my New Song Church family. Thank you for your love and support—every person who prayed and prophesied over this book and every person who took the time to encourage and ask how things were going—you have no idea.

And to my little Beau. I will never forget sitting down at dinner after being asked to submit a book proposal and posing a question to the whole family, "What should Mom write a book about?" to which you quickly responded, "You should write a book for parents and show them how to teach their kids to be salt, light, love. And you should make a kid's book to go with it." I knew in my spirit that God was speaking through you. Always use your voice for kingdom purposes. I love you, little brown-haired girl.

ABOUT THE AUTHOR

SARAH BLOUNT HAS devoted her life to sharing the story of God's wonderful goodness. After delivering her son Felix, stillborn, in 2012, she started her blog, *10K Reasons*, and God birthed in her a passion for communicating His Word. She has helped many women who have lost babies find comfort in choosing gratitude over grief. In September 2015 Sarah and her husband, Josh, stepped out in faith, moved to a new land, and pioneered New Song Church in Oklahoma City, where they copastor and desire to see people come to personally know God. Sarah is also the founder of HIS, a ministry designed for women who prize being found in Christ. Sarah and Josh have been married for sixteen years and have three larger-than-life children—Gus, Beau, and Sunny.

AUTHOR WEBSITES

Visit sarahblount.com for more parenting resources, curriculum for women's small groups, new blogs, and audio messages. You may also view Sarah's current speaking schedule or find information about inviting her to speak.

Visit 10kreasons.wordpress.com to view Sarah's online diary as she chose gratitude over grief and set out to

216

find 10,000 reasons to give thanks over the course of 365 days. This is an excellent resource for any mothers who are grieving the loss of a baby.

Visit newsongpeople.com for information on New Song Church. Josh and Sarah founded New Song and currently pastor the thriving church located in Oklahoma City.

CONNECT WITH SARAH
ON SOCIAL MEDIA:

Instagram: sarah_blount

Facebook: Sarah Newsom Blount

NOTES

CHAPTER 1: WHY WE CAN'T RETREAT

1. Julie Compton, "'Boy or Girl?' Parents Raising 'Theybies' Let Kids Decide," NBC News, July 19, 2018, https://www.nbcnews.com/feature/nbc-out/boy-or-girl-parents-raising-theybies-let-kids-decide-n891836.
2. Compton, "'Boy or Girl?' Parents Raising 'Theybies' Let Kids Decide."
3. Brandon De Hoyos, "Sexting Laws in the United States," Lifewire, April 15, 2019, https://www.lifewire.com/sexting-laws-in-united-states-1949957.
4. "Teenage Sexting Statistics," GuardChild, accessed July 7, 2019, https://www.guardchild.com/teenage-sexting-statistics/.
5. "Teen and Young Adult Internet Use," Pew Research Center, accessed April 4, 2019, https://www.pewresearch.org/millennials/teen-internet-use-graphic/.
6. "Talking Points on Porn: Statistics," National Center on Sexual Exploitation, accessed July 7, 2019, https://endsexualexploitation.org/statistics/.

CHAPTER 2: FAITH OVER FEAR

1. F. C. Cook, ed., *The Holy Bible According to the Authorized Version (AD 1611), With an Explanatory and Critical Commentary and a Revision of the Translation, by Bishops and Other Clergy of the Anglican Church*, vol. 1, part 1, Genesis–Exodus (New York: Scribner, Armstrong & Co., 1873), 253.
2. Bible Hub, s.v. "Exodus 1," accessed July 7, 2019, https://biblehub.com/commentaries/cambridge/exodus/1.htm.

3. Blue Letter Bible, s.v. *"towb,"* accessed July 7, 2019, https://www.blueletterbible.org/lang/Lexicon/Lexicon.cfm?strongs=H2896&t=KJV.

4. Bruce H. Lipton Ph.D., "Are You Programmed at Birth?," Heal Your Life, August 17, 2010, https://www.healyourlife.com/are-you-programmed-at-birth. See also T. S. Sathyanarayana Rao, M. R. Asha, K. S. Jagannatha Rao, and P. Vasudevaraju, "The Biochemistry of Belief," *Indian Journal of Psychiatry* 51, no. 4 (2009): 239–41, https://doi.org/10.4103/0019-5545.58285.

Chapter 3: Three God-Given Gifts for Parents

1. Bible Hub, s.v. "2 Timothy 1:7," accessed July 7, 2019, https://biblehub.com/commentaries/2_timothy/1-7.htm.

Chapter 5: How We Are to View Our Children

1. "Ancient Weapons: The Bow and Arrow," Women in the Bible, accessed July 10, 2019, http://www.womeninthebible.net/war-in-the-bible/bow-arrow-ancient/.

2. Brian Hertzog, "Craftsmanship: The Lost Art," October 22, 2015, https://www.brianhertzog.com/blog/craft.

3. Matthew E. May, "The Best Sushi Chef in the World," Quality Digest, February 28, 2013, https://www.qualitydigest.com/inside/quality-insider-column/best-sushi-chef-world-022813.html.

4. "Ancient Weapons," Women in the Bible.

5. "Ancient Weapons," Women in the Bible.

6. "Ancient Weapons," Women in the Bible.

Chapter 6: Our Role as Parents

1. Blue Letter Bible, s.v. *"gibbowr,"* accessed July 10, 2019, https://www.blueletterbible.org/lang/Lexicon/Lexicon.cfm?strongs=H1368&t=KJV.

2. David Guzik, "Study Guide for Judges 6," Blue Letter Bible, accessed July 10, 2019, https://www.blueletterbible.org/Comm/guzik_david/StudyGuide2017-Jdg/Jdg-6.cfm?a=217011.
3. Tom Kersting, "Media Kit," accessed July 10, 2019, http://tomkersting.com/wp-content/uploads/2017/12/Media-Kit-Tom-Kersting.pdf.
4. This quote is often attributed to Mark Twain, but its origin is actually unknown. See Quote Investigator, "Two Most Important Days in Your Life: The Day You Were Born and the Day You Discover Why," accessed July 10, 2019, https://quoteinvestigator.com/2016/06/22/why/.

Chapter 7: Salt of the Earth

1. 1 Won't You Be My Neighbor? "You don't have to do anything sensational for people to love you. What did Mister Rogers...," Facebook, July 25, 2018, https://www.facebook.com/watch/?v=172372716783790.
2. The Phrase Finder, "Worth One's Salt," accessed July 10, 2019, https://www.phrases.org.uk/meanings/worth-ones-salt.html.
3. The Phrase Finder, "Worth One's Salt."
4. Harvard Heart Letter, "Take It With a Grain of Salt," Harvard Health Publishing, November 2006, https://www.health.harvard.edu/heart-health/take-it-with-a-grain-of-salt.
5. James L. Lewis III, MD, "Overview of Sodium's Role in the Body," Merck & Co., accessed July 10, 2019, https://www.merckmanuals.com/home/hormonal-and-metabolic-disorders/electrolyte-balance/overview-of-sodium-s-role-in-the-body; Kristen Unger, "The Effects of Dehydration on the Cardiovascular System," Live Strong, accessed July 10, 2019, https://www.livestrong.com/article/150464-the-effects-of-dehydration-on-the-cardiovascular-system/.

6. Jon Johnson, "How Long You Can Live Without Water," Medical News Today, May 14, 2019, https://www.medicalnewstoday.com/articles/325174.php.

7. David Joachim and Andrew Schloss, "The Science of Salt," Fine Cooking Issue 119, accessed July 10, 2019, https://www.finecooking.com/article/the-science-of-salt.

8. Kimberly Y. Masibay, "Salt Makes Everything Taste Better," Fine Cooking Issue 91, accessed July 10, 2019, https://www.finecooking.com/article/salt-makes-everything-taste-better.

9. Joachim and Schloss, "The Science of Salt."

10. Masibay, "Salt Makes Everything Taste Better."

11. Masibay, "Salt Makes Everything Taste Better."

12. Masibay, "Salt Makes Everything Taste Better."

CHAPTER 8: LIGHT OF THE WORLD

1. *Merriam-Webster*, s.v. "identity crisis," accessed July 10, 2019, https://www.merriam-webster.com/dictionary/identity%20crisis.

2. Kevin DeYoung, "Jesus, Friend of Sinners: But How?," The Gospel Coalition, March 4, 2014, https://www.thegospelcoalition.org/blogs/kevin-deyoung/jesus-friend-of-sinners-but-how/.

CHAPTER 9: LOVE (GOD)

1. SWNS, "Americans Check Their Phones 80 Times a Day: Study," *New York Post*, November 8, 2017, https://nypost.com/2017/11/08/americans-check-their-phones-80-times-a-day-study/.

2. Michael Winnick, "Putting a Finger on Our Phone Obsession," dscout, June 16, 2016, https://blog.dscout.com/mobile-touches.

3. Kevin McSpadden, "You Now Have a Shorter Attention Span Than a Goldfish," *Time*, May 14, 2015, https://time.com/3858309/attention-spans-goldfish/.

4. Kesava Mandiga, "The Simple Truth About Technology and Human Attention Spans," Medium, May 16, 2018, https://medium.com/flock-chat/the-simple-truth-about-technology-and-human-attention-spans-311154c20fd.

5. John Calvin, *Institutes of the Christian Religion*, trans. Henry Beveridge (Edinburgh, UK: Calvin Translation Society, 1845), ch. 11, accessed July 10, 2019, http://www.ccel.org/ccel/calvin/institutes.iii.xii.html.

Chapter 10: Love (Others)

1. Msgr. Charles Pope, "A Brief Treatise on the Fruits of the Holy Spirit," Archdiocese of Washington, January 27, 2013, http://blog.adw.org/2013/01/a-brief-treatise-on-the-fruits-of-the-holy-spirit/.

2. *Merriam-Webster English Language Learner's Dictionary*, s.v. "adapt," accessed May 8, 2019, http://www.learnersdictionary.com/definition/adapt.

Chapter 11: Doers of the Word

1. *Standards for Accreditation of Baccalaureate and Graduate Nursing Programs* (Washington, DC: Commission on Collegiate Nursing Education, 2018), 24, viewed at https://www.aacnnursing.org/Portals/42/CCNE/PDF/Standards-Final-2018.pdf.

2. UC Education Marketing, "Top 5 Benefits of a Hands-on Learning Approach," Universities, Colleges & Schools.com, April 29, 2018, http://www.universities-colleges-schools.com/top-5-benefits-of-a-hands-on-learning-approach.

3. Bible Study Tools, s.v. "*Maher-shalal-hash-baz*," accessed July 10, 2019, https://www.biblestudytools.com/dictionary/maher-shalal-hash-baz/.

4. Blue Letter Bible, s.v. "*Shĕ'ar Yashuwb*," accessed July 10, 2019, https://www.blueletterbible.org/lang/Lexicon/Lexicon.cfm?strongs=H7610&t=KJV.

5. Blue Letter Bible, s.v. "*Yĕsha'yah*," accessed July 10, 2019, https://www.blueletterbible.org/lang/Lexicon/Lexicon.cfm?strongs=H3470&t=KJV.

CHAPTER 12: GREATER IS HE WHO IS IN YOU

1. David Guzik, "Study Guide for 1 John 4," Blue Letter Bible, accessed July 10, 2019, https://www.blueletterbible.org/Comm/guzik_david/StudyGuide_1Jo/1Jo_4.cfm.

2. Blue Letter Bible, s.v. "*kŏlyō*," accessed July 10, 2019, https://www.blueletterbible.org/lang/Lexicon/Lexicon.cfm?strongs=G2967&t=KJV.

Made in the USA
Columbia, SC
04 February 2024

31460835R00134